Risk Management for Company Executives

MANAGEMENT BRIEFINGS

EXECUTIVE BRIEFING

Risk Management for Company Executives

JOHN SMULLEN

FINANCIAL TIMES
Prentice Hall
An imprint of Pearson Education

London New York San Francisco Toronto Sydney
Tokyo Singapore Hong Kong Cape Town Madrid
Paris Milan Munich Amsterdam

PEARSON EDUCATION LIMITED

Head Office:
Edinburgh Gate
Harlow CM20 2JE
Tel: +44 (0)1279 623623
Fax: +44 (0)1279 431059

London Office:
128 Long Acre
London WC2E 9AN
Tel: +44 (0)20 7447 2000
Fax: +44 (0)20 7240 5771
Website: www.business-minds.com

First published in Great Britain in 2000

ISBN 0 273 65008 4

British Library Cataloguing in Publication Data
A CIP catalogue record for this book can be obtained from the British Library.

10 9 8 7 6 5 4 3 2 1

Typeset by Boyd Elliott Typesetting
Printed and bound in Great Britain

The Publishers' policy is to use paper manufactured from sustainable forests.

About the author

John Smullen BSc (Econ), MA, MSc (Econ), MBA was educated at the London School of Economics, Birkbeck College London and the London Business School. He has taught economics and in particular financial economics at a number of academic institutions. He is currently Senior Academic Advisor at the University of Greenwich, visiting Lecturer at the DeMontfort University and the Economics University of Cracow and Visiting Professor at the Catholic University of Uruguay.

He has also been a senior finance officer at Abbey National Plc, a major UK retail bank, being centrally involved in financial research, in particular, in relation to customers, products, business units, new business ventures, performance measurement, and budgetary and capital budgeting.

Since 1994 he has run John Smullen Consultancy and Training which has undertaken a wide range of consultancy and training projects mainly concerned with the banking industry. Among the banking organisations which John has undertaken work for are: the Royal Bank of Scotland, the Britannia Building Society, First Active, the Romanian Institute of Bankers, a Uruguayan Banking consortium, the Associacion de Marketing Bancario Argentino and the State Investment Bank in Equador the CFN. He has also worked for a number of training companies including the Chartered Institute of Management Accountants and Croner Training. John has also been involved in work for local authorities and charities on the financial and management issues in relation heritage management. In 1996 he became involved in the issues in relation to the pricing of taxis and has provided financial modelling services on this issue to a number of clients.

John has been a frequent contributor to conferences and has been the keynote speaker at a number of international conferences in Sidney, Helsinki, Brussels, New York and Buenos Aires. His publications include *Financial Management Information and Analysis for Retail Banks* for the Chartered Institute of Bankers in conjunction with Woodhead Publishing and *Balanced Scorecards and Activity Based Management* in the Financial Times Prentice Hall Management Briefings series. He also expects to publish *Transfer Pricing for Financial Institutions* with the Chartered Institute of Bankers and Woodhead Publishing by early 2001.

John can be contacted at:

Swan Cottage
Church Road
Stoke Hammond
Bucks MK17 9BP
Tel: 01525 270200
Fax: 01525 270946
E-mail: sj24@gre.ac.uk

Acknowledgements

I would like to dedicate this book to Nonie my sainted Aunt who died in 1999, a woman of unfailing good humour who sacrificed so much for my benefit.
I would also like to dedicate this book to the person whom I most admire and look up to, my wife, Marion.

Contents

Preface

In 1530 Atahuallpa had conquered the Inca Empire after winning a civil war with his half-brother, Huascar. He had control of the centre of what he thought to be the civilised world. He let a force of 100 footsoldiers and 60 horsemen led by Francisco Pizarro meet him at Cajamarca. The town was surrounded by Atahuallpa's army of 40 000 soldiers and he went to see Pizarro with 80 nobles and 6000 warriors. The Spaniards attacked the party, killed 6000 – 7000 Indians and captured Atahuallpa. A ransom was subsequently agreed which would exchange Atahuallpa for a room full of gold. The ransom was delivered but Atahuallpa was killed and the Inca Empire was conquered by the Spanish.

This story is apocryphal but illustrates many important insights that can be vital in understanding risk in relation to business. Events whose probability are very low do on occasion happen – lightning does strike. The self-confidence that comes with success may make leaders and organisations blind to risk. Authoritarian leadership often results in unresponsive and brittle organisations when that leadership is removed. New technology can have devastating impacts – the weapons (steel and gunpowder) and horses of the Spanish were a very important element in their military success. Alliances and relationships which are based on coercion may prove transitory. It may be difficult to understand and predict the behaviour of individuals and organisations which have radically different cultures and modes of operation.

It is a facetious suggestion that Atahuallpa might have prevented the Spanish conquest of the Inca Empire if he had read the rest of this book. There are risks which will not be adequately considered by any individual or organisation. Economic and political organisations have a cycle of life and death irrespective of the levels of success that they achieve. There are limitations in any analysis or associated policy in relation to risk. However a risk management system will ensure that certain risks are more adequately managed.

Risk management will not eliminate all risks. It will, however, enable a more effective management of those risks which can be identified and understood, although there will be risks for all organisations which they can neither identify nor understand.

The purpose of this book is to enable executive managers to understand the vocabulary of risk and their obligations to deal efficiently with establishing effective risk management systems for their organisations. It does not attempt to make managers expert in any of the components of risk, but it will allow them to understand the nature of relevant specialisations and how they may be used in organisational terms.

The comprehensive management of risks by organisations is in many ways a development of the 1990s, yet a number of the components of risk management have a long and important history. The insurance industry has focused on the management of risk for hundreds of years. Much of the initial analysis and the systems for operational risk management were developed by the military, and some of the first web sites in relation to operational risks that I visited were those of the US military. Organisations which deal with nuclear material and hazardous chemical and biological material have in their focus on safety developed risk management techniques. Health and safety is of its very nature a branch of risk management. The computer industry has also concentrated on managing what are a specific set of operational risks. Portfolio managers who developed their activities in line with Markov's Portfolio Theory fashioned in the early 1950s established some of the basic principles for market risk management. Banks have always had credit risk management as a key skill that they need to apply in their activities. Central banks and international financial organisations have devoted much of their activity to ensuring the stability of the financial systems. All these different approaches will be considered to some extent in this book, but the focus will be on a high-level view of risk with the identification of the role of specialists and their skills.

Although the primary focus is on commercial organisations, the material will be useful for non-commercial organisations both in the not-for-profit and the government sector. The projects in the UK to celebrate the millennium, which were sponsored by the National Lottery, illustrate the diverse range of risks which government and the not-for-profit sector may face. The Millennium Dome, which cost in excess of $1 billion, was dogged by risk-related issues in terms of the management of the project for efficient delivery, and it also had a pronounced public relations risk associated with the fact that the expenditure was on a structure with an apparently limited life span. Thus the diversity of risks which we will consider is relevant for any type of organisation.

In general, the words business, organisation and firm are used as interchangeable in the text and refer mainly but not exclusively to commercial organisations.

This book has benefited from the help and assistance of my many acquaintances whom I have met in work and social contexts. The ones who had most impact on this project are Andy Jesson, John Haynes, David Withey, Alan Swift and Andy Keddie. I would also like to thank Azlina Mohamed Noor Beg for her help and assistance in researching material for this book. Most importantly I would like to thank my wife for her support. The mistakes are mine and I would crave forgiveness for them. Any comments on the book are welcome on my e-mail address at SJ24@gre.ac.uk

Section 1

Introduction

1

Introduction – the nature of risk

WHAT IS RISK?

Risk relates to situations in which the outcome is uncertain and the benefits or costs of the different possible outcomes are not identical. An organisation which is subject to risk should be interested in the management of risk where the differences in benefit or cost of the different outcomes is significant. This provides a wide definition of risk and risk management.

There is an orthodox distinction in finance theory between risk and uncertainty. The term risk is applied to a situation in which the outcome is unknown but the probability distribution from which the outcome is drawn is known. Uncertainty is related to a situation where neither the outcome nor the distribution of outcomes is known. The term uncertainty may also be used in situations where the outcomes may not even be identifiable. The nature of the outcome is usually expressed in financial terms.

The distinction between risk and uncertainty can be illustrated by a number of simple examples. The outcome of the roll of a die will be a number from one to six inclusive. Each number (all things being equal) will have a probability of one in six of being the outcome. The resulting probability distributions are illustrated in Figure 1.1. This is a situation where risk applies. Before the die is thrown we do not know what the outcome will be, but we do know how likely it is that any particular number will be thrown.

Fig. 1.1 Example of risk distribution

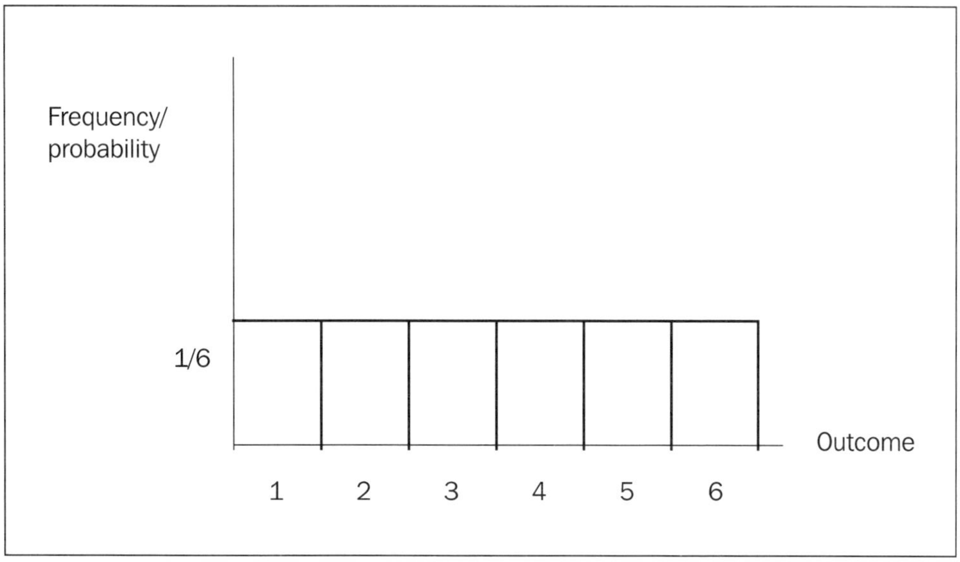

Consider a business which is trying to identify the possibility of a major problem in relation to public pronouncements by a key executive. Let us look at some public examples in relation to this type of problem. US president George Bush brought on many difficulties with his statement, 'Watch my lips, there will be no increases in taxes', thereby creating hostages to fortune. Perhaps the most dramatic example was when Gerald Ratner, speaking on 23 April 1991 at the annual convention of the Institute of Directors in London, described some of the products sold by his jewellery chain as 'crap'. In October 1987 the share price was 398p; by August 1992 it was 12p. Most of this decline could be attributed to the publicity relating to the statement and the reaction of his customers. A similar story relates to Glen Hoddle, manager of the England football team in the 1998 soccer world cup. He was interviewed about his religious ideas, particularly in relation to his use of a faith healer for the players and his views on reincarnation. The discussion gave the impression that he thought people with handicaps had received a judgement from God. As a result of the interview there was a public reaction to his views and he was forced to resign.

Is it possible to draw a diagram like Figure 1.1 to analyse these situations? The answer is obviously no. We cannot identify all the outcomes in relation to these issues and we have little idea of what would be the probabilities. However, these risks are always present since we can identify many examples of organisations which have had problems as a result of statements by their executives. These would be considered situations of uncertainty.

In this book we will look at situations of both risk and uncertainty as defined by finance theory, as it is important to consider both types of situation to be the subject for risk management policies. They form the basis for a sensible continuum of situations covered by risk management polices and illustrated in Figure 1.2. As one moves to the right over the continuum one moves to situations in which it is progressively more difficult to establish a sensible system of risk analysis and a comprehensive risk management policy.

Fig. 1.2 **Continuum of increasing risk**

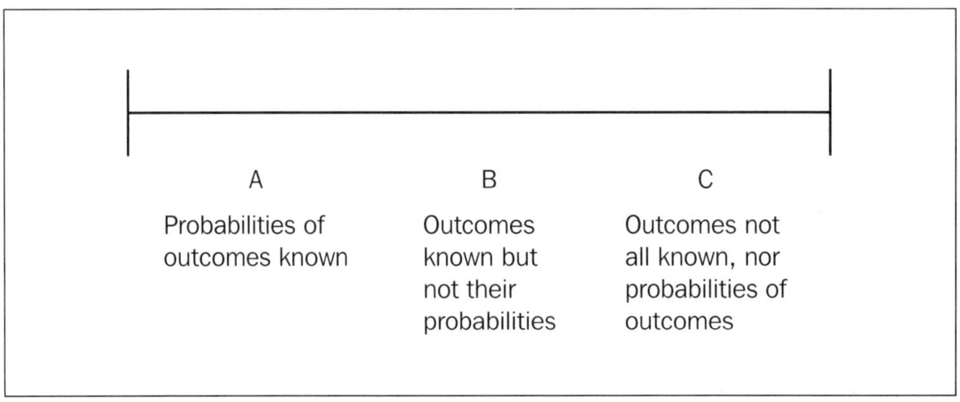

Category C illustrates one of the main problems in relation to developing a sensible risk management policy. There is an infinite number of possible risks that an organisation may face and it is impossible to identify them all. Part of the risk management process is trying to establish the different types of risk, but one should also consider how to prepare the organisation to cope with many unanticipated problems.

MEASURING RISK

The appropriate measure of risk depends heavily on the preferences of the individual organisation which is the subject of the risk. These issues of preference will be dealt with in Chapter 7. However, it is important to consider the normal measurement of risk. There are in essence two measures of risk which are the standard deviation of the distribution of returns and the worst case.

The role of standard deviation is illustrated in Figure 1.3. It is a measure of the spread of the distribution of returns. The flatter the distribution, the greater the standard deviation and the greater the risk. This measure of risk can be used to measure only those risks which fall most generally into category A as depicted in Figure 1.2; it is not appropriate for risk categories B and C. Considering Figure 1.3, above the standard deviation is a measure of the horizontal spread of the distribution, thus the risk depicted in 1.3 A is lower than in 1.3 B.

Fig. 1.3 Measuring risk by standard deviation

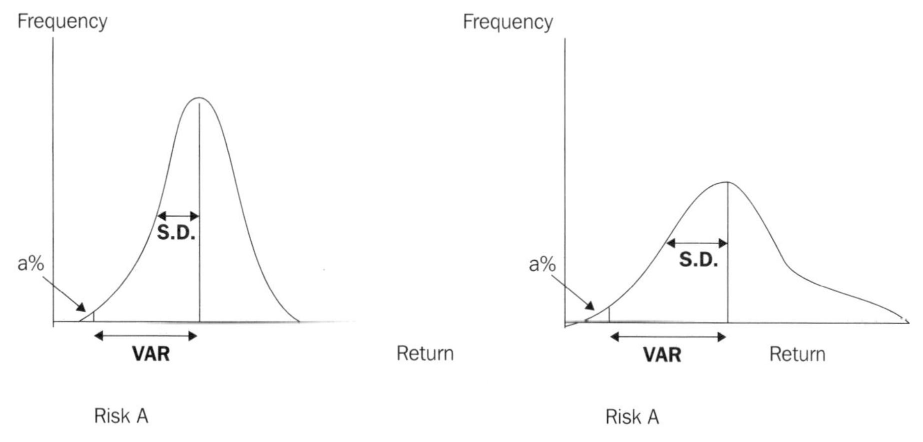

The second type of risk measurement is by worst case. This can be applied to both types of risk A and B as depicted in Figure 1.2 since if an institution can enumerate possible outcomes it can measure which represents the worst return. A variant of worst case which has become popular in measuring financial-related risks is value at risk (VAR). The VAR is the difference between the average return and the level of return at which returns will be worse only in a percentage of instances. VAR can be measured only where one is aware of the distribution of outcomes relating to a particular type of risk and thus cannot be applied to the risks identified by categories B and C of Figure 1.2.

There is an array of risk measures for the categories of risk identified by type A of Figure 1.2. In the situation where outcomes can be identified but not the probability of their occurrence, it is possible to identify worst case which therefore can be applied as a risk measure to risks of category B. Risks of category C cannot, by their very nature, be subject to any system of measurement.

WHY SHOULD ORGANISATIONS ESTABLISH RISK MANAGEMENT SYSTEMS?

There are in essence two types of answer to the above question. The initial answer is that the management of risk will better allow the organisation to fulfil its objectives. The secondary set of answers relate to the changing regulatory and environment standards in which organisations operate. Regulators, financial markets, and accounting standards bodies are increasingly focusing on the need for organisations to effectively manage risk.

All organisations are subject to risk. It is also important that organisations are prepared to take risks since they are in many ways the lifeblood of progress and productivity. The question is not whether an organisation should take risks but which risks it should take and on what terms. Risk management is in part about deciding this.

Portfolio theory, which is at the basis of financial economics, suggests that investors will put their money into a portfolio of assets to diversify away the risks involved in individual assets. It suggests investors may be interested in the risk profile of a business and how it fits with the general portfolio of their investments. Finance theory would seem to indicate that managers are more anti the risk in their business than their shareholders are. Shareholders use the risks of a business to diversify their holdings while managers find the diversification of this risk more problematic.

How does this perspective fit with the examples quoted above? Shareholders in Ratners would certainly have preferred it if Gerald Ratner had not made his statement. If one considers the Ratners example in terms of a decision as to whether or not the chief executive should be flippant in public forums or not, it is, I suspect, obvious that it is financially beneficial to the organisation for him not to behave in this way. Risks should be taken only on the basis that they generate sufficient rewards for the organisation.

Whatever the nature of the organisation, taking risks should be considered and undertaken only if they are worthwhile within the set of objectives of the organisation. Risk management policy is ensuring that this is the case.

The regulatory environment in which many organisations operate increasingly focuses on the need for organisations to manage risk appropriately. The Turnbull Report (1999) prepared by a working party of the Institute of Chartered Accountants in England and Wales has been adopted by the London Stock Exchange and will form the basis for the requirements on internal control systems. The international banking regulations established through the Bank of International Settlements in Basle has since 1988 imposed increasingly sophisticated and comprehensive requirements for the risk management of the banking system. The process for obtaining grants from the various UK Lottery funding authorities is now demanding a risk evaluation and policy for any major award. There is a very definite increase in pressure on all organisations to have a greater understanding of the risks they face and a policy which will enable those risks to be managed. This process is gaining strength in all the countries of the developed world.

EXAMPLES OF ORGANISATIONS WHICH HAVE HAD PROBLEMS MANAGING THEIR RISKS PROPERLY

This section gives examples to illustrate that there are very diverse types of risks that organisations take and that if they are not carefully considered they can have disastrous impacts for both the organisation and the individuals responsible for the decisions. That these risks are very common can be seen from Table 1.1, which is taken from *The Independent*, published in London on 25 January 2000. It was a newspaper taken at random for a particular date and these are the risk articles contained in that edition. The sheer diversity and number of articles should give some indication of the importance of risk management issues for business. We have also included a number of infamous examples of business-related risks where the results turned out badly for the organisations concerned.

The 'Hitler Diaries'

The publication of the 'Hitler Diaries' was one of the great publishing embarrassments of the 20th century. The diaries were purchased in 1981 for publication in the German magazine *Stern* for DM 85,000 each. The deal was struck without the benefit of any scrutiny of the documents by a handwriting expert, forensic scientist or historian. Rupert Murdoch, the media tycoon, bought the UK, Commonwealth and US rights for $1.2 million after Lord Dacre, the historian, attested that the diaries were genuine. *Stern* published the world exclusive on 22 April 1983 and almost contemporaneously received the results of forensic tests which judged the documents to be fake. *The Sunday Times* in

London published the story on 24 April amid controversy as to the documents' authenticity. The diaries were undoubtedly fake.

Perhaps an amusing postscript to the story is its implications for the *Sunday Times*, a Rupert Murdoch publication, which gained an extra readership of 60 000 for the story, of which an estimated 20 000 remained loyal to the paper. *Stern* had to repay the $1.2 million that Murdoch had paid for the publication rights and is said to have lost DM 19 million over the diaries.

Table 1.1 **Business risk management stories from *The Independent*, 25 January 2000**

Dorling Kindersley lost £14 million – it printed 13 million copies of 'The Phantom Menace' but sold only 3 million in association with the latest Star Wars Film.
LRC sued for £120,000 in regards to faulty condoms.
The Trans Tec ex-accountant accuses Geoffrey Robinson of improperly claiming government grants.
Katie Dawson, governor of Risley Prison, alleges widespread sexual discrimination.
The management of Tolworth Hospital accused of abandoning elderly patients to a bullying regime.
Mitterand and friends alleged to have used Elf to spread millions in bribes worldwide.
26 killed in South African bus crash.
The abolition of duty free for travel within the European Union hits Eurotunnel.
EMI shareholders disappointed with terms for merger with Time-Warner.
Vodafone could claim victory with less than 50% of Mannesmann.
Predicted power struggle between new Marks and Spencer chairman Luc Vanderveld and Peter Salsbury, the chief executive.
Euro falls further against sterling in wake of G7 talks.
NatWest bolsters defence by lifting share buy-back to £3.5 billion.
Leaks of P&G/Warner Lambert bid 'create an environment in which we cannot continue meaningful discussions'.
Computers can't solve skills crisis.
Clariant bids £1 billion to keep out BTP rivals.
Article suggestion sale of Thistle Hotel shares.

Chicago Board of Trade

The Chicago Board of Trade (CBOT), one of the world's most important financial markets, was brought to a standstill in April 1992 due to a flood in the tunnels below the Chicago business district. The problems affected power and telecommunications. The operation was temporarily moved to a 'hot site' in Northbrook, Illinois, 35 miles away, and just six hours after the disaster CBOT was open for trading again.

Visa

In the *Sunday Times* of 16 January 2000 there was an article headlined 'Hacker gang blackmails firms with stolen files' which alleged that Visa was subject to a £10 million demand from hackers in December 1999. The article suggested that hackers stole computer 'source codes' and threatened to crash the entire system of Visa, a giant of the credit card industry, which handles transactions by 800 million cards held worldwide. A Visa spokesperson was quoted: 'We hardened the system, we sealed it and they did not return. We have firewalls upon firewalls but are concerned that anyone got in.'

Savings and loans

In the years between 1980 and 1993 1300 thrift institutions failed in the United States. Their failure was a combination of a number of factors, most notably a rise in interest rates above their previous historical levels and an unsatisfactory regulatory environment. In particular their main purpose was to provide fixed interest rate loans for domestic house purchase which was funded by variable rate borrowing. The final bill for unwinding the crisis was $300 billion.

Flu vaccination

In the late 1970s there was a health scare created by a single case of swine flu in the United States. Since this was the strand of flu which had been responsible for the epidemic that swept Europe in 1918 and had caused widespread fatalities, this led the US government to initiate a wide programme of vaccination. When the United Kingdom was faced with the same problem, it decided to wait and see. There was no epidemic, but the vaccine used in the US had some unfortunate side-effects and led to a number of civil cases for damages. The UK enjoyed the most beneficial outcome, but it took public health risks which were thought unacceptable in the US.

In all these instances where the outcomes in relation to risks are judged to be unacceptable for an organisation, it is easy to specify how it might have avoided the outcome by sensible policies. Then it needs to identify possible risks and policies which will mitigate those risks. It then needs to be decided whether the policies of risk mitigation are sensible. To successfully implement a risk management policy and system is far from easy but in many of the examples above the institutions could have avoided problems with a more sensible attitude towards risk.

CLASSIFYING RISKS

The examples quoted in the last section illustrate the diversity and complexity of the risks which a business may face. In general, business-related risks can be divided into three categories: market risk, credit risk and operational risk. There are many possible categorisations in relation to risks. The definitions in relation to market and credit risk are straightforward, while that for operational risk is very wide. Many commentators divide operational risk into a series of categories, and we will consider each of these separately.

Market risk

Market risk relates to variations in the value of financial contracts. The core focus in relation to market risk is obligations traded on financial markets. Market risk is not related only to the financial contracts that businesses enter into that are traded on financial markets, but also to the impacts in business performance as a result of changes in prices in financial markets. Thus, for example, a firm may be dependent on interest rates and exchange rates and their impacts on its general business irrespective of any impacts on traded financial contracts. If one considers the sale of Rover, the British car manufacturer, by BMW, it was very much motivated by the exchange rate between sterling and the euro over the course of 1999. The key components in relation to market risk for business are outlined in Table 1.2.

Table 1.2 Components of market risk

Prices	*Financial instruments*	*Business activity*
Equity values	Short-term debt instruments	Revenue flows
Interest rates	Bank debt	Cost flows
Exchange rates	Long-term debt instruments	Profitability
Commodities	Equities	Present value
Indices	Derivatives	

The key to market risk is that changes in the prices in financial markets can have impacts on the financial performance of a business. The main financial market prices relate to the value of companies' shares or equity values, the interest and exchange rates, commodity prices, and indices of the major financial markets. Changes in these prices have two types of impact on the value of a business – they may impact on the value of financial obligations into which a business has entered, and they may have an impact on the level of business generally.

Credit risk

Credit risks relate to the possibility that a counterparty to a financial transaction will not fulfil their obligations. In the main it has related to whether a debt to a business will go bad and not be honoured. Whether a business trades on financial markets or not, it is likely, as a by-product of its operations, to extend credit to its customers. Thus credit risk and its management is an essential aspect of any business.

There are other financial obligations not necessarily related to lending, as for example in relation to derivatives contracts which will have a credit risk associated with them.

Operational risk

Operational risk is often seen in terms of the risks in relation to the activity of the business. However, in recent times it has become progressively a catch-all category of risk which incorporates all types of risk which are not market or credit related. Although this categorisation is not entirely satisfactory, it is the one which will be adopted in this book. The sheer diversity of risks which can be incorporated in this category can be seen in Table 1.3, which is taken from a presentation by David Withey, chief executive of Amelia Financial Systems, which specialises in operational risks for the banking sector. This represents his attempt to specify all the different elements which might form categories of operational risk.

It is always difficult to look at a list and identify whether it has omissions or not. There is, however, one important risk category which does not appear to be included in David Withey's list and that would relate to general business risks. To take a simple example, if one is considering a business plan there are a number of risks which will need to be taken into consideration. The results may be very sensitive to various assumptions and, for instance, one needs to consider issues of volume forecasting, price forecasting, cost forecasting, operational and financial gearing. These types of business risk would fall within the category of operational risk. Reviewing Table 1.3, it may be possible to include these issues in relation to business risk as part of problems in relation to inadequate management information. However, the nature of the different categories and the extent to which the categories have overlapping edges is a matter of nuance. The table nevertheless represents a starting list or check list in relation to operational risk.

Table 1.3 Different categories of operational risk

Events and security	Supplier
Transactions	Human resources
Information security	Theft and fraud
Inadequate management information	Change management
Legal and regulatory	Loss of reputation
Information systems	Technology

The category of risk which for banking organisations is probably covered by David Withey's list but has not been explicitly considered as it should be for other types of organisation, is product risk.

HOW ANALYTICALLY TRACTABLE ARE THE DIFFERENT TYPES OF RISK?

In one of the earlier sections we reviewed the different types of risk and their analytical tractability in terms of the extent to which the possible outcomes and their distribution was understood. The more readily the possible outcomes and their distributions are understood, the easier it is to apply statistical analysis to the understanding of risk and the framing of risk management policies. In general, market and credit risks are more likely to be statistically tractable and have been the subject of statistically based systems for identification and analysis.

There is a body of mathematical and statistical techniques for understanding these risks. The use of mathematical techniques for certain types of operational risk depends on the type of risk. In relation to the consideration of engineering risks, for example, there is an elaborate and articulate numerical discipline for risk management. A number of banking institutions – notably Bankers Trust – have applied the value at risk methodology to operational risk and argue that this may be sensible, particularly where institutions share information so that a sufficiently large database can be created for analysis. An example of this would be the sharing of information between different banking institutions on the details of fraud.

Figure 1.4 is an illustration of my view of the nature of the different categories of risk and the extent to which they are analytically tractable. Market and credit risks are of a nature that their outcomes and the probability distribution of their outcomes is more easily understood than is the case with operational risks. There are, however, for all the different types of risks some risks which will prove very difficult to model within any statistical framework: this is the case particularly with some operational risks.

Fig. 1.4 The nature of different categories of risk

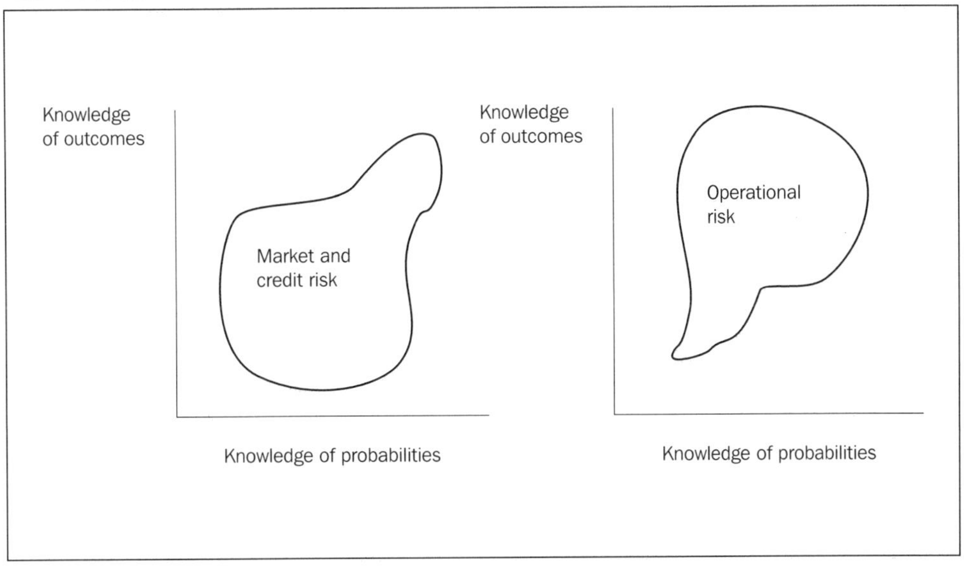

There is a danger which must be considered in the establishment of any risk quantification and management system. Individuals are better at understanding the problems of which they have had experience or which their technical training gives them tools to deal with. There are many disciplines which deal with aspects of risk management analysis in relation to the treasury function, accountancy, auditing, engineering, and so on. One must try to take the widest perspective, and although one should make use of the relevant skills it is important to take a more comprehensive view than that adopted by any particular background or discipline. One must always be on guard against new and unexpected dangers and uncertainties.

CONCLUSION

History indicates that all organisations have a cycle that runs from birth to death and over that life cycle they are subject to a number of risks. It may be impossible to ensure organisational immortality, but many of the risks to which firms are subject can be managed. If one considers the major problems of organisations, many of them can be avoided through sensible risk management. Risk management is thus a sensible and valuable activity for any enterprise.

Section 2

Understanding the nature of risk

2

Understanding the nature of risk

INTRODUCTION

This chapter attempts to outline some of the more important concepts in terms of an overall understanding of the nature of risk and its management. It is not an attempt to present a technical discussion of all the issues, but rather a discussion of the important ideas which executives need to understand if they are to be able to adequately manage the overall process of risk management. It is a guide to enable you to discuss and understand the activities of the risk-related professionals.

FORECASTING AND RISK MANAGEMENT

If one could predict the future there would be no need to worry about the uncertainties of the world, since there would be no uncertainties. It is important that all organisations make their decisions with a view to what will happen in the future, but they must have an understanding of the limitations that any forecast may be subject to. Evaluating the likely levels of error in forecasts is a problematic exercise. There may be a discipline of econometric forecasting where all the estimated equations are subject to statistical measures of how likely they are to be prone to errors, but in general these measurements should not be taken too seriously. One must be sceptical of the success of economics as a forecasting discipline.

What determines the success of forecasting

In this world nothing is certain. There are many different techniques for forecasting the future, ranging from the qualitative evaluation of possible situations to the use of complicated statistical and mathematical models. The outputs of some models are forecasts of the most likely future to visions of a range of possibilities. Often forecasts and targets in business are just different sides of the same coin. Management by their actions are expected to influence the future. There are a range of factors which influence the degree to which a situation can be forecast, and we will consider these below.

The degree to which past experience can be used

In business there are decisions of which the organisation has extensive experience and decisions which are organisationally unique. In general, the former are more predictable than the latter. To draw from my experience of the retail banking industry, if the interest rate changes in the economy and a bank is considering how it should change the rates of interest on its retail products, it will consider issues such as the market in which its products are sold, the possible actions of competitors, and the impacts between the products which the bank offers. Since interest rates change regularly, the bank will have extensive experience of the relationships involved, so it will be able to predict the impacts of its policy with some degree of confidence. If, on the other hand, one considers the decision to launch a product which is totally new to the marketplace and of which the bank has no past experience, prediction is more difficult.

I have been involved in two such product launches where the product was highly innovative in the market to which it was directed. In one case the product was five times more successful than expected and in the other case the product was one-fifth as successful in comparison with expectations. In the second case the re-evaluation on the basis of scenarios had scenario titles such as 'one-eighth of target'. Therefore the degree of past experience may be a central factor in determining the levels of predictability in a particular situation.

The volatility of the environmental situation

The more volatile a particular situation, the more difficult it is to predict the future. To take the example of sovereign risk, if an investor is considering the alternatives of investing in the United States or in Zimbabwe, there are obvious differences in the ability to forecast the levels of returns which may be obtained or the possibility of total loss of the investment. The political, economic and financial environment in the US is much more stable than that in Zimbabwe and therefore can more easily be forecast.

The levels of understanding of the issues

There are some problems which are better understood than others. If one considers a comparison of forecasting competitor reactions in a given situation or the probability of default on a particular consumer loan for a finance company. The behaviour of firms in oligopolistic industries has always been problematic for economists. The theory of games has just multiplied the myriad intellectual frameworks within which the analysis can be conducted. It is thus sometimes very difficult to predict competitor behaviour. If, on the other hand, we consider predicting losses on consumer lending, the techniques of credit scoring and performance scoring which have developed since the 1960s allow the prediction of account delinquency with some degree of accuracy. There are thus some situations which are simply more intrinsically easy to predict.

The nature of the situation to be forecast

Predicting in some situations appears more intrinsically difficult than in other situations. Financial economists, for example, have developed an interesting argument to explain their inability to forecast prices in financial markets. This argument is best illustrated in terms of a simple example related to the exchange rate between the dollar and the euro and is illustrated in Figure 2.1. It can in principle be applied to most financial markets but may require a degree of modification. The figure illustrates the movement of the exchange rate through time. At time **t0** the price is **t0x**. If at this point in time all the market participants decide that the market price at **t1** will be **t1y**, how will the price move from one price to the higher price? There are three price time paths, of an infinite number of possibilities, which are illustrated as **a**, **b**, and **c**. The price path which one would expect the market to follow is that indicated by **a**. The reason for this is that the holders of dollars would wish to hold on to dollars until the higher price is achieved and buyers of dollars would wish to purchase immediately at the lower price, thus supply declines, demand rises, so the price will rise.

Fig. 2.1 **The predictability of price in financial markets**

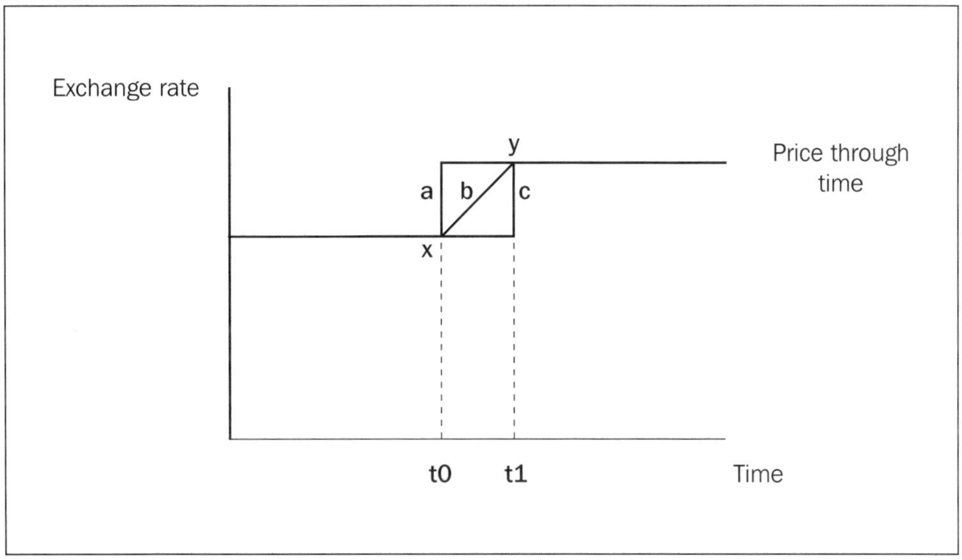

This process can be characterised more generally. If new information which has an influence on the market price becomes available to market participants it will immediately be incorporated into the price. By a similar argument all the information available at any point in time will be incorporated into price formation. Thus prices change as a result of new information. New information is likely to have a random impact on future prices, so if current information is incorporated in price, today's price is the best estimate of the future price.

In applying this to many financial markets it can be modified to incorporate trends but it suggests that precise forecasting will have severe limitations. To illustrate what this means, one may take the example of the US stock market, where real returns over the period 1802–1996 were fairly constant at just below 7 per cent in real terms, but the market might fall by up to one third in a single year. There are market trends, but these provide only a broad framework within which to forecast.

Different forecasting techniques

The most commonly used standard methods of forecasting are the delphic method, non-quantitative analysis, statistical analysis and scenario analysis. The delphic method is simply to use expert opinion. This may take the form of asking internal or external experts to forecast a required future situation or using opinions in the public domain. One might, for example, use the government's economic forecasts and assumptions to forecast what will happen to the economy.

Non-quantitative analysis involves considering a situation and the factors which motivate it and using these as the basis for making predictions. One might, if one wishes to forecast levels of competition within a particular market, use the Michael Porter 'five forces' analysis technique which sees competition in terms of the behaviour of certain actual and potential players in any market situation – competitors, suppliers, customers, producers of substitutes, and new entrants. These types of non-quantitative analysis may be particularly useful in situations in which there are likely to be no runs of useful data, or in which situations are changing. If, for example, one wished to analyse the impacts of changing technology on a particular marketplace this might best be undertaken within a non-quantitative framework.

The quantitative methods for forecasting the future in general have their origins in economics or econometrics. They require a high level of technical competence to motivate them and their results are not uniformly satisfactory. It is interesting to note that Paul Ormrod in his book *The Death of Economics* (1994, Faber and Faber) describes how the results, in his wide experience of most large macro-economic models, are fudged to give results which appear to be intuitively acceptable. My own background is as a mathematical economist and I have come to the view that one should always apply a reasonableness test to the results of elaborate statistical analysis. If the numbers are consistent with one's intuitive view of a particular situation, one should accept the numbers. Where the forecasts conflict with one's intuition, one should review the techniques and the implications of one's forecasts. As a rule of thumb, in 90 per cent of these situations of conflict with intuition, intuition is likely to be more correct, and in 10 per cent the statistical techniques are more likely to be correct. However, these 10 per cent are very important because they provide insights which one did not have before and may be vital in increasing our knowledge of a particular situation.

Scenario modelling comprises establishing a model in relation to how a situation is determined and then making different assumptions to predict the outcomes. Scenario modelling is as useful as the structural properties of the model and the initial assumptions. It is commonly used by strategists and management accountants and again should be treated with a degree of scepticism. Scenario planning can be used to subject the key organisational assumptions to serious scrutiny in regards to any predictions about the future.

Forecasting techniques for business-related situations are far from entirely successful and therefore should be regarded with scepticism. Management often has a better understanding of the processes to be modelled than the individual modeller. One should always ensure that models are explained as far as possible in non-technical terms and not hidden behind technical expertise and jargon, so that more than the modeller's expertise can be applied to the problem.

Conclusions in relation to forecasting and risk management

Forecasting is an attempt to predict the future and in relation to business there is no uniformly foolproof method. However, some techniques in certain circumstances are more likely to be accurate than in other situations. Understanding the degree of uncertainty in relation to particular forecasts is very important. In fact, this level of uncertainty is related to the issues considered in the initial chapter. If one can forecast an outcome and the degree to which that forecast may be in error, it will help in organising risk management.

THE MEASUREMENT OF RISK

In Chapter 1 we provided an initial analysis of how risk might be measured. This section gives a more detailed exposition of risk measurement and how it might actually be motivated. The measurement of risk can be undertaken only in situations where one knows the distribution of probabilities of different outcomes or can identify all the different outcomes without a knowledge of the probabilities of their occurrence – risks of type A and B in Figure 1.2. If one cannot identify all the possible outcomes it is impossible to adequately measure risk, so category C in Figure 1.2 cannot in principle be measured, although one may have rough estimates of the approximate magnitude of certain risks.

In principle there are two different types of risk measure – one type looks at the variability of outcomes and the other type looks at some measure of bad events. The business or organisation may be interested in principle in the variability of outcomes as well as what happens when things go wrong – both are aspects of risk management.

Measurement of risk in terms of category A

In category A risks we know the range of outcomes and the probabilities of those outcomes. Risk measurement and management can be seen in terms of comparing distributions and deciding which is the most appropriate for an organisation.

Fig. 2.2 Category A risks and their measurement

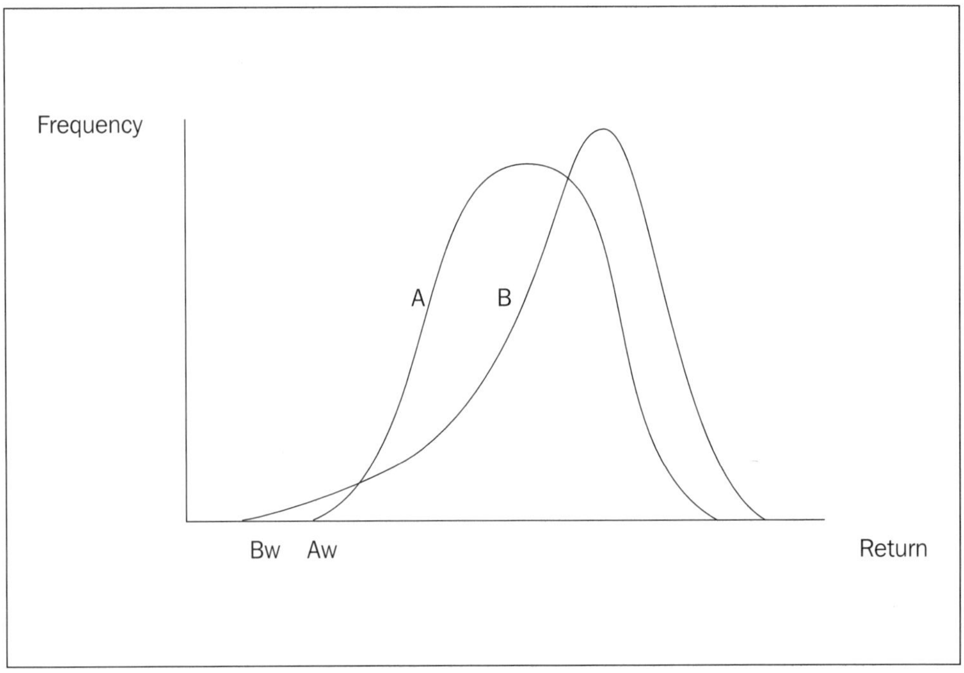

Figure 2.2 shows two different types of risk distributions, A and B. These relate given levels of return on the horizontal axis to different frequencies. They express risk in terms of returns, which is the most standard type of quantification of risk. In comparing the distributions, A has a lower-level average return than B.

In considering risk, whether one prefers A or B depends on how one weighs up the totality of the two distributions. Ultimately the decision by a manager or a firm may be in comparisons of the whole distribution. However, distributions can be described in terms of statistics which summarise the information described by the whole distribution. A normal distribution, for example, requires only two descriptive statistics – a mean and standard deviation. The mean is the average return and the standard deviation measures the spread of results around the mean – the higher the standard deviation, the more spread is the distribution. With a normal distribution the mean and standard deviation exactly and totally describe the distribution. If a distribution is not normal, as is the case with A and B in Figure 2.2, then these two measures may be insufficient to capture the precise nature of the distribution.

There are two types of risk measurement – those based on the spread of the distribution, such as standard deviation, and those which reflect some definition of bad outcomes, the two most common measures of bad outcome being worst case and value at risk. The worst case is represented by Aw and Bw in Figure 2.2. The value at risk can be seen as 'a worst case in normal circumstances'. As we explained in Chapter 1, it is the loss relative to the average return which will be exceeded only in a particular percentage of cases. In considering the distributions A and B in

Figure 2.2 from the perspective of risk measures, distribution B has a lower standard deviation than distribution A, but it has a worse worst case and in all likelihood a worse value at risk. Thus different measures of risk give different orderings in terms of these two distributions. The measure which is appropriate depends on the organisation which is using the measures, there is no obvious right ordering since the orderings may be based on different risk perspectives.

In risk management two plus two is less than four

One of the most important aspects of risk management is that when one combines a number of different risky situations, the level of risk is usually expected to decline. The reason for this is that when one risk has a bad outcome it is unlikely that the other risk will also have a bad outcome. This phenomenon is likely to be true irrespective of whatever types of risk are to be considered. This argument is illustrated in Figure 2.3. If one considers the time paths of returns for two types of investments or risks, A and B, they will vary with time. However, when A is doing well, B is doing badly, and vice versa. The combination of investment in both will give the time path of returns marked A + B, which is much less volatile. Combining risks in general reduces them. In fact, the conditions where risks are not reduced by combinations are very restrictive. These impacts pictured in Figure 2.3 are usually described as the benefits of diversification.

Fig. 2.3 Adding risks will lower them

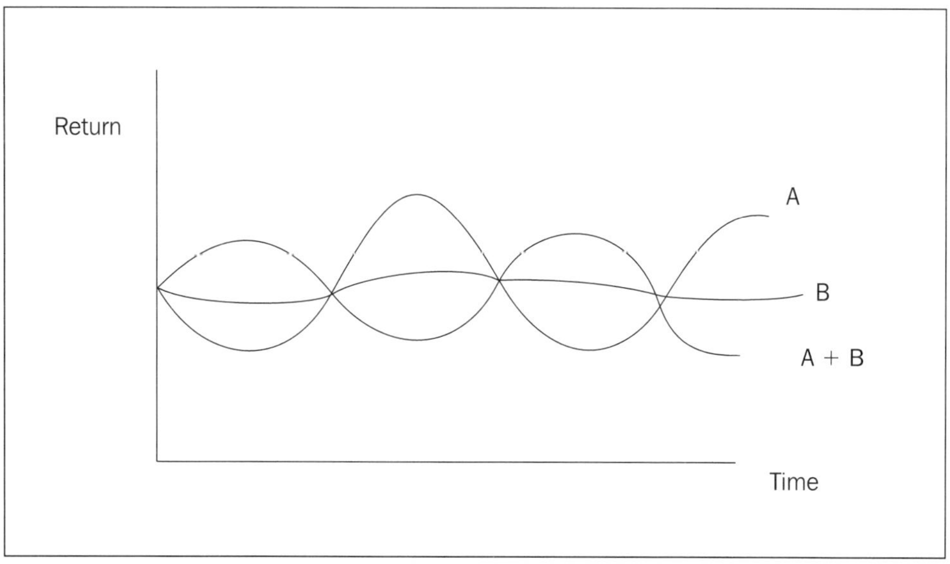

Measurement of category A risks

In the previous section we have assumed that the distribution of returns is known with some degree of certainty. There are many techniques in risk management that assume that these distributions can be calculated. This section reviews the ways in which these risks can be calculated and discusses the reliability of those calculation techniques. These techniques are usually applied to situations in which there is a quantity of data on the risks under consideration.

If one considers data in relation to the returns on financial obligations such as shares, bonds and derivative securities traded on the financial markets, these would be examples of risks for which the requisite data may be collected, so the above measurement techniques can be applied to financial market obligations. There are other examples where there is sufficient data to apply these analytical techniques, for example in relation to different types of credit risk, in relation to bank lending or general company solvency evaluation. We shall develop the argument in terms of portfolios of financial obligations, but these ideas can be transposed to other situations where appropriate.

Historical data

If an organisation has a portfolio of financial obligations which can continuously be valued in financial markets, it can estimate the returns on that portfolio over past time periods. It can, for example, calculate the daily returns it would have made over the past year if it had held its current portfolio and from that calculate a distribution of daily returns. The resulting estimated distribution can be used to evaluate the risk in the current portfolio.

The virtue of this type of analysis is that it does not impose any statistical regularities on estimates. However, it reflects the experience of a particular historical period and that may not be the situation in which we are currently operating. During the late 1990s the stock markets in the Anglo-Saxon world rose and had a relatively low volatility in comparison with what happened in 2000 when the volatility of share prices, especially in high-tech industries, increased dramatically. Risk measured on the basis of data for the late 1990s will be lower than is indicated by stock market behaviour in 2000. There is always a question of how relevant history is.

Variance/co-variance measures

If a portfolio is made up of a number of different obligations, as for example shares, the mean and variance of the portfolio can be estimated from the mean and variance of the returns of the individual obligations. The problem with this methodology is that it imposes the assumption of normality on the distribution of returns and this assumption is unlikely to be valid especially if the portfolio contains any substantial element of derivative obligations. It is thus likely to underestimate risks if the portfolio of obligations has any significant element of derivatives. The estimation of the distribution of returns in this instance is also based on historical experience and is only as relevant as the historical data on which it is based.

Monte Carlo simulation

Monte Carlo simulation is becoming progressively more important as a method of understanding the nature of financial market risks which organisations face. The most sophisticated software for analysing interest rate risk is currently based on Monte Carlo simulation. As explained above, simulation is the establishing of a model which on the basis of initial conditions and assumptions will forecast the future. In the case of Monte Carlo simulation the model is run with many different sets of assumptions to give a number of end results. One may, for example, make thousands of separate calculation runs on the basis of different assumptions. The initial assumptions are drawn randomly from some distribution of possible values which is specified as part of the modelling process. The result is a distribution of final outcomes. The resulting estimate of the distributions of returns is only as good as the structure of the model and the specification of the distributions in relation to which the assumptions are randomly drawn. However, these models can accommodate worries that the historical experience does not adequately encapsulate the risks of a particular situation, as might be the case with stock markets over the past few years.

The measurement of category B risks

If we can outline the outcomes but do not know the probabilities of the different outcomes, it is still possible to develop some measures of risk. The two measures which can be employed are those relating to the worst case and the difference between the best and the worst case.

Worst case scenario modelling

One of the ways in which organisations attempt to understand worst cases they face is through scenario modelling. This is to produce a model which allows them to see what will be the impacts of the worst case they face. The models of which I have had most experience relate to the estimation of worst cases in relation to portfolios of mortgages. They consider the financial impacts of certain levels of defaults on loans and the implications of realising the collateral to the loans. One can then consider particular scenarios which are drawn from considerations in relation to possible financial crises, as for example what happened in the US housing market in the period after the 1929 stock market crash, or what happened to the UK housing market in the recession from 1988 to 1992.

If one is not content that historical experience will provide sufficiently representative worst cases, one might wish to construct the impacts of a hypothetical crisis. Let us take as an example the possibility of a financial crisis on the international capital markets. Since the 1970s derivatives have become a major element in the workings of the capital markets, as have more recently computer-based trading systems, and we have limited experience of how these changes might impact in times of financial crisis. There were capital market crises in 1987 and 2000, but these cannot be compared with the all-embracing crisis of 1929. Thus, if one is to consider worst cases, one may wish to develop scenarios which are not entirely historically based. These models form the basis for measurement of risk by scenario.

HEDGING

Hedging is lowering risk by holding more than a single risky situation. It is highly likely, in this instance, that the risks will to some extent offset each other. The basic ideas are illustrated in Figure 2.3 where the two time paths of risky returns can be combined to eliminate some of the variability of the two different return profiles. The same point is made from another perspective in Figure 2.4 which considers the position of two assets which an investor holds. The using of the example of two assets is just for illustrative purposes – it can be applied to any risky situation. The performance of the two assets is measured in terms of an average return which is depicted on the vertical axis, while risk is measured on the horizontal axis. The measure of risk employed can be standard deviation, value at risk or worst case. The conclusions as to the ability to hedge are the same irrespective of the definition of risk, although the numerical expression will differ for different definitions of risk.

The risk-return combination of the two assets is marked **A** and **B**. Asset A has a higher level of risk and return than asset B. The curved line between **A** and **B** represents the risk-return portfolio made up of holding combinations of the assets A and B. Since there are combinations which involve lower levels of risk than that of B, the less risky asset, it can be seen that hedging by holding both assets lowers risks. The nature of the line between **A** and **B** will depend on the degree to which the returns of A and B vary relative to each other. If better returns for A coincide with poorer returns for B and vice versa, the greater will be the risk-reducing impacts.

The degree to which a situation can be hedged thus depends on putting together portfolios which have elements whose variations are, to some extent, inversely related. Since few situations vary exactly together, the combination of situations is likely in nearly all cases to reduce risk. There are some situations which are exactly inversely related and others where they are exactly directly related. In the former case it may be possible to eliminate risk entirely. The most important examples of these situations relate to the impacts of derivative products on financial markets. This is why derivatives can be vital in financial risk management.

CONCLUSION

This chapter has outlined the different definitions of risk and how they may be measured. In essence, if one can specify a risky situation it is likely to be possible to measure the extent of the risk. The degree to which risk can be measured depends on the usefulness and reliability of the data and the extent to which we can understand the problem. We have also considered the aggregation of risks and how they might be hedged. This is an important case since it is core to the problem of what attitude a business should have in deciding whether a given return is sufficient compensation for taking a particular risk.

Fig. 2.4 Risk return combinations

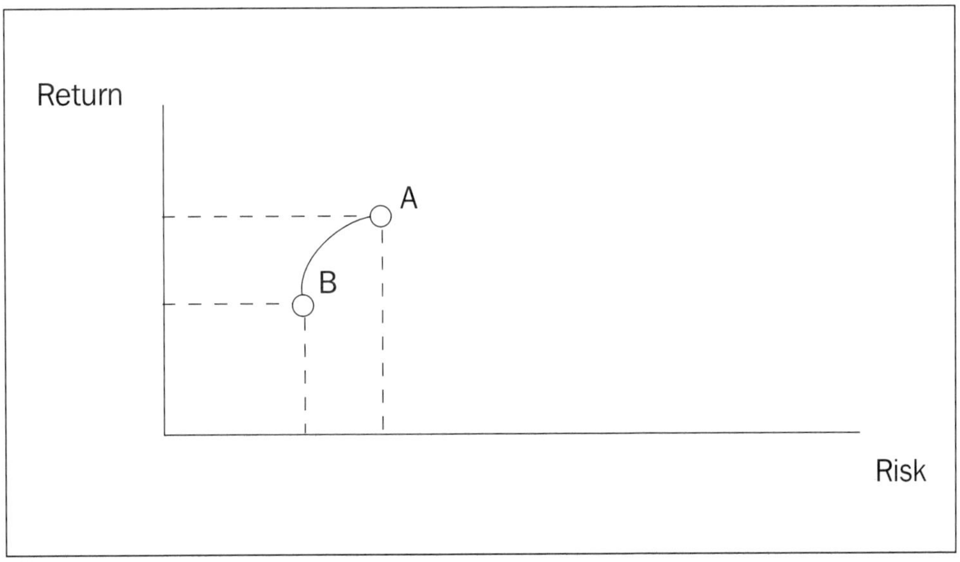

3

Operational risk

INTRODUCTION

There are many different categorisations of risks and definitions of operational risk. In general, market and credit risk are easily definable and separable from other types of risk. This is not the case with operational risk. In this book we will use the most general definition of operational risk as those risks which do not fall into the categories of market and credit risk. The implication of this definition is that there is a wide range of different risks which fall within the same category. The techniques for dealing with operational risks depend on the specific risk under consideration and some are the subject of extensive bodies of knowledge while for others there is great uncertainty and no standard treatment. There are a number of different definitions of operational risk and it does not matter which is adopted as long as there is an appreciation of the whole range of possible risk-related issues for an organisation.

OPERATIONAL RISKS CAN BE MAJOR RISKS

If one considers the totality of risk in a business, they relate to how that business behaves over time. They relate to the cash flows of the business, its profitability, and its value as a business. If one were to ask which of these is the most important, one would tend to focus on the value of the business and in particular the value of the business to the shareholder. For most businesses the variability of its shareholder value will best be explained in terms of operational risks. That the impacts of operational risk can be extensive can be seen from the information in Table 3.1 which is drawn from the web site of Robert Tomski Associates.

This table is illustrative rather than comprehensive but indicates the possible magnitudes of individual operational risk problems. Although many of the problems listed are related to issues of financial obligations and markets, the problems are intrinsically those of operational risk. The first three listed of greatest magnitude, for example, are all related to issues of organisational control rather than credit or market risk issues. The illustrations do, however, have some elements related to other risk categories.

Table 3.1 Examples of operational risk losses

Institution	*Activity*	*Date*	*Magnitude US$bn*
Credit Lyonnais	Poor lending control	1980/90s	29
UK Life Insurance	Pension mis-selling	1988–94	18
US banks, corps, retailers	Cheque frauds	1993	12
US Federal Aviation Authority	Delays in systems development	1994	2.7
Sumitomo Corp. London	Copper trading	1985–96	2.6
Orange County	Bond trading	1994	1.7
Daiwa Bank, New York	Bond trading	1984–95	1.4
Barings, Singapore	Futures	1995	0.8
London Stock Exchange	System cancellation Taurus	1993	0.7

TYPES OF OPERATIONAL RISK

The identification of operational risk is a difficult task for any organisation, given that it is seen in terms of the factors which will cause variations in organisational value. It covers a wide diversity of possibilities. This is the category of risks which we will in general find most difficult to identify and to measure. It will also present issues over what is the best way to deal with this diversity of risks. There is an established toolkit for dealing with market and credit risk and although there is some debate as to its general nature, most practitioners have the same ideas about best practice. In the case of operational risk there are some facets which have been the subject of extensive analysis and where there are established methods for dealing with risks, as for example in engineering, quality control and insurable risks. There are in these instances best practice bodies of knowledge that can be deployed but this is not the case with all categories of operational risk, as for example in reputational or legal risks. Therefore in this chapter we have included a number of perspectives which will give both a flavour of the different approaches and an ability to cross-check as to whether one has sensibly identified all the risks to which a particular organisation may be subject.

There is an important distinction to be made in understanding operational risk and it provides some answer to the problem that not all risk can necessarily be identified. It is the distinction between the causes of risk and the resources in the business which are at risk. It is not always possible to enumerate and analyse the sources of risk, but it is in most instances easier to identify the assets which are at risk and how one may protect them. There is a statistic, the veracity of which I have been unable to verify, that 50 per cent of the businesses affected by the explosion in the World Trade Centre in New York went out of business in the aftermath of the terrorist attack. Part of the reason for this will have been lack of adequate disaster contingency planning. One may not be able to enumerate all the possible causes for a business facility to go out of operation, but one can postulate how the facility can be replaced in the aftermath of such a catastrophic event. Thus, in some instances risk management can be about having in place plans in relation to problems with particular business resources even if the exact cause of the problems cannot be identified.

There are many different classifications of operational risk and in considering the identification of these types of risks it helps to consider a number of classification frameworks. We will consider three which are in common usage as illustrations that give a flavour as to the categories of operational risk one may wish to consider. The first system is replicated from the opening chapter and was produced by Amelia Financial Systems as part of the classificatory work to establish operational risk management software. It is depicted in Table 3.2. This is a comprehensive classificatory system but as observed earlier it does not consider many of the issues in relation to general business-related risks. If, for example, a business is considering its strategy on a major capital investment, this classification will not consider all the problems which might be encountered. It is thus based on a less general definition of operational risk than that on which this chapter is based.

Table 3.2 Categories of operational risk

Events and security	Human resources
Transaction risk	Theft and fraud
Information security	Change project management
Control frameworks	Loss of reputation
Inadequate/incomplete management information	Technology
Legal and regulatory	
Information systems	
Supplier	

The second risk classification is one taken from PricewaterhouseCoopers. It divides operational risk into two categories – operations risk and business event risk. These titles can be a little confusing. Operations risk is composed of transactions-related risks, problems in relation to operational control, and technology systems risks. Business risk is the broader risks from an organisation's day-to-day operations. Table 3.3 outlines the PwC categories of risks. This is a set of operational risk categories which are used in application in the finance industry and in particular in banking. In considering these distinctions, Barclays, as quoted in an article entitled 'Risk management's final frontier' in *Euromoney*, September 1996, believes that operational risk is responsible for 30 per cent of the bank's earnings volatility, the other 70 per cent being due to changes in the levels of their provisions for bad and doubtful debt.

Table 3.3 PricewaterhouseCoopers' operational risk

Operational risk	Business risk
Transactions risk	Business/event risk
Execution error	Currency convertibility risk
Product complexity	Shift in credit rating
Booking error	Reputation risk
Settlement error	Taxation risk
Commodity delivery risk	Legal risk
Document/contract risk	Disaster risk
	Regulatory risk
Operational control risk	
Exceeding limits	
Rogue trading	
Fraud	
Money laundering	
Security risk	
Key personnel risk	
Processing risk	
Systems risk	
Programming error	
Model/methodology error	
Mark-to-market error	
Management information	
IT systems failure	
Telecommunications failure	
Contingency planning	

Table 3.4 gives another perspective to the definition and categorisation of operational risk. It is taken from the risk management system developed by Bankers Trust. To give a little background into banking risk management systems, bank regulators are worried about the possibility of banks collapsing and wish to see risk management systems in place which lower the probability of insolvency. They wish to see that the bank has sufficient risk capital to cover the potential problems related to the specific nature of their businesses. The risk capital is defined broadly as the shareholder funds of the bank.

Table 3.4 Bankers Trust's categories of business operational risk

Risk category	*Functional responsibility*	*Example*
People	Business line Human resources Security	Human error Internal fraud Staff unavailability
Technology	Business line technologies Central infrastructure Data centre	Failure of technology Virus damage Loss due to antiquated systems
Relationships	Sales and marketing Business management Legal Compliance	Legal disputes Contractual disputes
Physical assets	Operations management	Loss of physical environment Business interruption Loss of negotiable assets
Other external and regulatory	Business line compliance Regulatory Security	Regulatory change External fraud

The regulatory authorities set the required capital in relation to a particular configuration of businesses. In recent years banks have sought to replace some general regulatory multipliers with their own analytical models to specify the required capital. The regulators have allowed internal models to be used for market risk but have been uneasy about this type of modelling for credit, and particularly operational risk. Banks generally have more confidence in credit risk modelling than in operational risk modelling. The bank which is recognised to be at the forefront of operations risk modelling is Bankers Trust. It argues that with a combination of database creation, using the opinions of experts, and quantitative modelling it is possible to estimate distributions of returns in relation to operational risk. The categories of operational risk which it employs for its operational risk analysis are outlined in Table 3.4. The table is adapted from *Risk*, October 1996.

RISK IDENTIFICATION

These schema for categorising operational risk identified in the previous section provide a background for the process of risk identification which we will consider in more detail in the more practical section of the book. They provide ideas and categories which will allow an organisation to check that it has identified the more obvious practical examples of risk. But every organisation is different and thus will need to be treated individually, although there will be distinct similarities between businesses in the same industry. Therefore some of the schema will provide a good framework for banking organisations.

The two main techniques for identifying risks that one can use are to consider the business from the perspective of the value chain or to consider risk issues in terms of business assets at risk and ways in which those assets are at risk. The value chain analysis consists of considering enterprises from the perspective of the strategic capabilities which generate value. It is a strategy-based focus that identifies risks in terms of the key processes and activities of the business. An example of this perspective comes from the KAI Corporation Risk web site which sees risk in terms of the supply chain, which is the process leading from inputs to outputs offered by the firm to the marketplace. The analysis identifies risk by mapping supply groupings to business process or product groupings.

Table 3.5. gives some methodology. It is a good way of associating a strategic perspective to risk management.

Table 3.5 **Operational risk examples drawn from supply chain analysis by KAI Corporation Risk**

Issue	*Risk*	*Consequence*
Water failure in manufacturing plant	Failure of infrastructure to provide sufficient clean water	Manufacturing delayed or stopped completely
Corrupt data from external source for financial transactions	Erroneous or failed data processes	Bad or no transactions – loss of customer confidence
Key supplier unable to provide goods for supermarket	Supermarket unable to sell goods	Loss of customer and transfer of loyalty to another supermarket
Power supply glitches	Business unable to continue	Shareholder and customer confidence lost
Call centre service insufficient	Dissatisfied clients and customers	Customer confidence and sales decrease

The 'what is at risk?', 'how is it at risk?' methodology consists of establishing categories in terms of both these attributes and can be pictured in terms of a matrix structure, as shown in 3.1. This technique was initially developed by the US military and has been modified as a procedure for risk identification by a number of organisations, most notably the Institute of Chartered Accountants of England and Wales, for a business setting. The categories along the horizontal and vertical axes can be established by brainstorming but the standard set of categories is illustrated in Figure 3.1. They may not be an exhaustive classification of risk factors but they are a good place to start and can be added to as the organisation increases its knowledge and sophistication in the understanding and management of risk. This technique is developed in more detail in Chapter Eight.

Fig. 3.1 Identifying operational risk

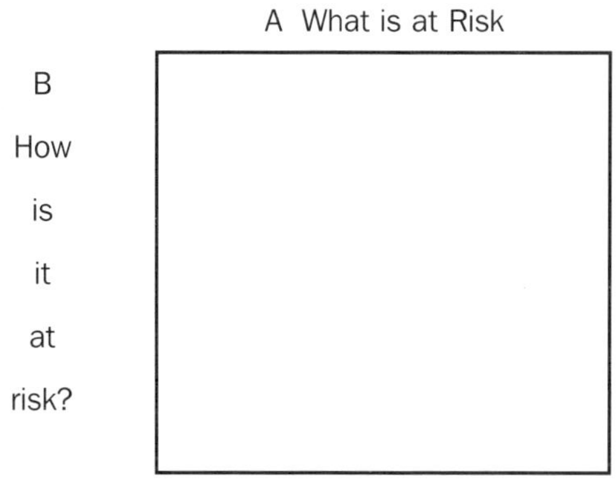

A What is at risk?

Reputation
Products
Inputs
Customers
Employees
Physical assets
Financial assets
Systems
Knowledge
Capabilities

B How is it at risk?

Gearing
Organisation
Products
People
Processes
Environment

BUSINESS RISKS

In general in most of the schema for dealing with operational risk outlined above there is little concentration on the normal risks which businesses face in terms of variability of sales and costs – the items which are usually dealt with by a business's budgetary variance reporting. The last schema, the risk matrix, does make some attempt to deal with these issues in looking at issues in relation to gearing and the general economic environment. That a business should be interested in all the factors which may influence its value can be seen easily by a consideration of orthodox finance theory. Finance theory suggests that the evaluation of any decision in business should be undertaken in terms of calculating the present value of a decision and if the present value is positive this will give financial support to undertaking the action indicated by the decision. The most difficult aspect in calculating the present value of a decision is not the forecasting of the decision cash flows, though that may be problematic, especially in relation to forecasting revenues, it is usually the decision in relation to the rate of discount to be applied to the cash flows. At the highest level of generality the rate of interest should reflect the risk involved in a particular decision, but the exact quantification of this rate may be technically and practically complicated.

The establishing of rates of return on decisions is one of the most important aspects of a comprehensive and sensible risk management system.

THE LEVELS OF UNDERSTANDING OF OPERATIONAL RISK

In Chapter 1 we divided the understanding of risks into three categories – A, B and C – to distinguish the degree to which we understand a particular type of risk. With category A risks, one knows the range of outcomes and the distribution of probabilities in relation to those outcomes. In the case of category B, the outcomes were known but their likelihood was not known. In the case of category C risks, a business was not sure if it was able to enumerate all the possible outcomes.

In considering the range of risks identified in this chapter it is not obvious which categories of risk each one naturally fits into. The different types of risk which fall within the category of operational risk are more diverse than their counterparts of market and credit risk. This debate has been seen within the banking community where Bankers Trust has argued that many core risks are quantifiable, particularly if different institutions are prepared to pool their data. In the area of fraud, for example, competitors in the banking system have long been prepared to share experiences. The development of benchmarking systems where consultants have created databases in which the exact source of information is masked from the competition has formed precursors for sharing data on an anonymous basis. The Bankers Trust view has not received general approval in the industry or from the regulators, but it has I think, provided a convincing case that some operational risks are of category A.

Many operational risks are process or engineering related, and quantitative risk assessment has been an important engineering discipline associated in many cases with health and safety. The one in a thousand million failures per hour is standard for flying control systems in modern aircraft. Quality control has provided quantification of certain operational risks over a number of years. Cost-benefit analysis has been applied to issues in relation to expenditure on transport safety – relating probabilities of fatalities to expenditure on projects which will save lives. In general, an improvement which saves lives with a certain probability is given a monetary value and is set against safety expenditure.

There are many reservations and criticisms of these quantifications, which can be illustrated by a quote, cited in *Accident and Design* by B. Toft, edited by Christopher Hood and David K.C. Jones, published by UCL Press. It is the reply by the Comptroller General of the US to Senator Mike Gavel in relation to the confidence that could be placed in predictions of the possibility of nuclear accidents: 'As far as we could learn during this brief review, DoD and Nasa officials can offer little guidance as to how very rare failures or catastrophic accidents to systems can be anticipated, avoided or predicted ... Nasa goes to extraordinary lengths – reliability costs is hardly an object – to prevent disasters in manned vehicles ... Still three astronauts were lost in one vehicle. The Soviets suffered similar losses in other attempts. No one can tell if and when such catastrophic failures will be repeated.'

The quote indicates that there are many systems whose risks can be analysed in terms of component failures but the results cannot be used to evaluate the reliability of the whole system.

The example of atomic disasters such as Three Mile Island and Chernobyl illustrate that systems which are in essence built to be fail-safe may lead to disasters which are unanticipated. The question is, how do we consider risks which have very low probabilities but very high potential impacts? There are two issues in relation to these situations – how reliable we consider the estimates to be, and what weight we give to them in policy-making terms. The answer to the first question may vary with particular instances, as for example we may be able to estimate the probability that a plane will crash-land on a processing centre with some degree of accuracy, but the impacts and risks of new technologies, for example those associated with biological engineering, may be more difficult to estimate.

An interesting survey of operational risk undertaken by Airmic and Lloyds in 1999 identified the levels of concern of businessmen in relation to operational risk. They tried to identify the types of business risks which organisations were most worried about. The results are given in Table 3.6. Given the lack of problems which Y2K created, it is interesting to speculate whether this list should be taken too seriously.

Table 3.6 Airmic/Lloyds survey on lack of cover for business risks

Loss of reputation	34%
Y2K failure	30%
Brand/trademark	25%
Intellectual property erosion	21%
Terrorism	9%
Climatic	7%
Credit risk	7%
Class action	5%
Currency risk	5%
Claims against directors and officers	2%
Genetically modified organisms	2%
Employee stress claims	0%

CONCLUSION

Within the schema of this book operational risk is defined as a catch-all category that covers all risks which are not market or credit risks. It is a diverse category and covers some types of risk that are well understood and amenable to statistical analysis and can be dealt with by standard tools. There are, however, risks that are operational which are difficult to identify and which we do not entirely understand. Thus operational risks are some of the most problematic and difficult for an organisation to deal with. Operational risks have been responsible for some of the largest and most prominent business failures in recent years. It is thus important for an organisation to be able to identify and deal with operational risks.

4

Credit risk

INTRODUCTION

Credit risk is the risk associated with the non-payment of financial obligations to which an organisation is entitled by other parties. It can be viewed in terms of a number of perspectives. Most organisations, as part of their activities, extend credit to other parties and this is particularly the case with their customers. The risks associated with these loans are a major element in credit risk. If an organisation is extending credit to another party, it is possible that the creditworthiness of that party will vary through time, and any variation can also be seen as an aspect of credit risk. Payment delays may not lead to a default by the counterparty, but they again are an aspect of credit risk. To extend the preview of credit risk to its most exotic limits, there are credit risks in relation to financial derivatives. In essence, financial derivatives are financial obligations (explained more comprehensively in the next chapter) which are traded on financial markets or over the counter, usually termed OTC between financial institutions. Where they are traded on financial markets the market operations are set up to minimise the problem of a party to a contract defaulting. In the case of the OTC markets there is no general arrangement for minimising credit risk and the organisation which enters into a derivatives transaction will be subject to a credit risk from the party on the other side of the transaction.

EXAMPLES OF CREDIT RISKS

History is littered with examples of credit risks going bad. A good friend of mine was rung up at 1 am to be told by his company secretary that Barings was going bust and that his company would follow. Barings was their most important debtor. When Barings was eventually taken over by ING my friend threw the most munificent 'I'm not bankrupt' party at the corporate entertainment facility of a major football club.

Looking at the past few decades there have been many world economic problems associated with credit risk. The Opec-inspired rises in oil prices at the beginning and end of the 1970s led to oil-producing countries having massive surpluses to invest. The international banking system invested these 'petrodollars'. The investments proved to be bad for a number of reasons, among them the rising interest rates in the international economy, and led to great structural instability for the international banking system. In particular they led to the debt crises in Latin America and with the communist economies of eastern Europe. The early 1990s saw the Japanese property and equity markets collapse, which led to very high levels of bad debt for the Japanese banking system. In 1996, the Economist Intelligence Unit estimated the levels of bad debt in the Japanese banking system to be in the region of $500 billion. Subsequent estimates have put this level much higher, at some $715 billion.

Between 1980 and 1993 1300 thrifts and 1500 banks failed in the United States. We have already discussed that the failures in the thrifts or savings and loans were in the main related to interest rate risk and the rise in interest rates. But there were other issues related to these failures, and one major aspect was to do with credit risk. In particular, loans related to the energy and property sectors were major drivers in the banking problems during this period.

Let us look at some specific examples. The Continental Illinois bank, which failed in 1984, had $1 billion of bad debt losses. These losses were strongly related to problems in the energy sector and in particular falling oil prices led to a deterioration in the levels of collateral in relation to its loans. In reviewing the failure of Continental Illinois, Professor Shelagh Heffernan, Professor of Banking and Finance, City University Business School, London, saw some of the major causes of the bank's problems in the following terms: a lack of a rigorous procedure for underwriting loans and thus an overexposure to poor-quality loans to the US corporate sector, the energy sector and real estate. The delay in classifying loans as non-performing led to the undermining of depositor confidence in the bank. More than 25 per cent of banking failures in the US in the late 1980s were related to banks based in Texas. Examples of Texan banks which received federal support during this period are First Republic Bank (1988), First City (1988) and Mcorp (1989). The problems in general stemmed from excessive concentration on lending to the energy sector, with property as collateral for the loans.

It is often difficult to put examples such as these within a single risk category since interest rates, commodity prices and operational problems are part of these stories. The examples of credit risk outlined in this section are all taken from the financial sector. This is due to the fact that banks have lending as one of their core products. It is interesting to note that the management of credit risk must be one of the core bank competencies, yet there is a multiplicity of examples of bank failure related to unwise management of credit risks. Although the management of credit risk is core to the banking industry, it is vital for numerous other businesses since they extend credit in some form or other to their customers.

EVALUATING CREDIT RISK

The evaluation of credit risk can be seen in relation to Equation 4.1 which considers the main issues in relation to the understanding of credit risks. It outlines that the level of expected losses E(L) is dependent on three factors: the probability that a loan will default **D**, the level of exposure **X** and the proportion of the obligation which can be recovered **(1 – R)**, in which R is the proportion recovered.

This perspective covers the main overall issues but does not adequately deal with issues over payment delay and problems where a debtor becomes less creditworthy over time. As with the rest of this section of the book the idea is to provide a basic knowledge of the issues an executive can depend on specialist support for an understanding of issues of systems or analytical detail.

Equation 4.1

$$E(L) = D^{*}X^{*}(1 - R)$$

The level of expected loss **E(L)** is a measure of what one would on average lose on a particular loan or by extending credit to a particular customer. In this section we shall use the term loan but we refer also to any situation involving the extending of credit. If one considers a loan portfolio, some loans will go bad but in general most will be entirely satisfactorily serviced by the debtor. The expected loss will be related to the proportion which do not service their loans. When an organisation initially provides the loan, it knows that some customers will go bad and some will fulfil their obligations. It may be aware that the performance of an individual loan can be predicted to some extent but that predictions will never be entirely successful. If one has a portfolio comprised of a large number of loans, Equation 4.1 will be a forecast of the levels of loan losses. If, on the other hand, we are considering a single loan, the loan will either go bad or not, so the level of losses will either be $X^{*}(1 - R)$ or zero. The expected level simply reflects the probability of default.

The evaluation of the expected levels of losses can be made when the initial credit is extended and subsequently to understand how the credit risk is changing. The forecasting of levels of losses is a form of identification of credit risk which is useful in determining the levels of return necessary to compensate for credit risk, in deciding whether to extend credit, and in deciding how to treat counterparties who have not adhered to the terms of the credit agreement.

MODELLING CREDIT RISK

The previous section outlined the main components in any evaluation of the levels of credit risk. The modelling of the components is very often organisational specific. Organisations will have a structure of categories which relate to potential recipients of credit and the risk of current debtors based on their payment behaviour. This section deals with the 'state of the art' methods of evaluating credit risk. If one wishes to consider these issues further, *Managing Credit Risk* by Caouette, Altman and Narayanan (1998, Wiley Frontiers in Finance) is an excellent source. The material in this section is taken to some degree from their work.

One can divide the problems into a number of types of potential debtors: large corporates, middle-market borrowers, middle-market private borrowers, small businesses, commercial real estate, residential real estate and consumers. The problems and analytical methods used for each of these borrowers will tend to be different. In general, the most sophisticated models and systems were developed in the banking industry and that is why this section focuses on best practice in the banking system. Some large businesses will use these types of techniques but for smaller businesses they will require simpler systems.

Large corporate borrowers

These organisations which have publicly traded debt and equity are forced by the capital markets and general regulations to provide the public domain with accurate and up-to-date information. They are also subject to extensive scrutiny by the financial press, the investment community and its researchers. Their obligations are likely to be credit rated by professional credit agencies which have continual links to the management of the organisation and its internal perspective. Models of credit risk in relation to these organisations tend to be based on publicly available information and the outputs of the rating agencies.

Middle-market borrowers

Publicly traded with moderate disclosure requirements, middle-market borrowers are unlikely to have publicly traded debt and thus are unlikely to be rated by agencies. Currently there is little use of credit-scoring models and much emphasis is put on their management and financial statement analysis.

Middle-market private borrowers

These have no publicly traded stock or debt, so there are limitations on the amount of information available on the business. This leads to reliance on financial statements and financial analysis of those statements. If a financial institution is doing the lending, reliance is on collateral and covenants. There is limited use of credit-scoring models for this type of customer.

Small businesses

There are information problems with small businesses in that accounts may be unaudited, and reliable financial information may be difficult to obtain. This means relying on close monitoring, covenants and collateral. There is some use of credit scoring. Attention should be paid to the key individuals in the business.

Commercial real estate

In general there is no publicly traded stock so risk taking depends on analysis of accounts, attention to key individual and projection of cashflows and collateral on any project.

Residential real estate

Here there is strong reliance on collateral values. In recent years there has been greater concentration on credit-scoring models.

Consumers

There are no financial statements, but the presence of credit referencing agencies ensures that there is comprehensive relevant data on borrowers. Reliance is on different types of demographic data. In this area there is extensive use of credit-scoring models.

This review is not entirely comprehensive and if one wishes to consider the diversity of modelling which has been applied to different levels of credit risk – which includes the use of expert systems (which seek to encapsulate the knowledge of seasoned professionals), neural nets, and stress-testing models – it is probably sensible to start with Caouette *et al*, cited above. The use of bank references and guarantees is also important in the case of many of these diverse types of bank customer groups.

A SYSTEM FOR MANAGING CREDIT RISK

This section will focus on the issues from the example of the banking system, but many of the ideas and techniques are applicable to any business. It will end by considering how these may be applied to an environment where credit risk is less central to an organisation's activity or, if the business is small, what credit risk policies it should consider.

Organisational culture

In all organisations there has been an increasing view over the past decade that shareholder value is the key objective for commercial businesses. There are many different ways in which shareholder value can be generated, but one of the key perspectives is to ensure that the organisational cashflow is as good as possible. If one considers some of the major banking organisations, they develop a credit culture that is core to the organisation and the generation of value. Developing a credit culture is central to extending credit in an effective manner.

Morgan Guarantee Trust

Morgan Guarantee has a very strong culture. It traditionally hired career professionals who were steeped in the culture of the organisation. William R. Barrett, Jr., managing director and Morgan's senior lending officer, North America, said: 'The bank has never had financial pressures for current income that would require us to take silly risks.' The culture is to ensure that one understands what lending risks will be undertaken by the organisation. New recruits have to be accepted by the whole group. The organisation depends on informal networks as a part of the decision-making process. Tradition and precedent are seen as vital guides to making any lending decision. There is a consensus culture and an emphasis of raising problems as early as possible.

Bank One

Bank One is generally considered to be one of the best managed and most innovative banks in the US. It has expanded by buying a number of banks and the problem for the lending culture has been to ensure that it pervades new units with a different culture and history. The culture has been established by the key leaders, the father and son John G. McCoy and John C. McCoy. The bank is very interested in knowing the customer. Its loan portfolio is comprised of small loans and when its customers have become sufficiently large to merit large exposures, Bank One has been prepared to pass these customers onto other banking organisations. The culture is to take some risks, and officers who do not have some problems in their portfolios are seen as lending too little. The early recognition of bad loans is also core to the culture.

These case studies exemplify a number of principles that the leading decision should be subject to sensible judgement processes. If there are problems with loans, they should be recognised early, so the performance of loans should be monitored constantly. The portfolio should be considered as a whole and there should be limits to overexposure.

EXTENDING CREDIT

The process for extending of credit depends on the situation one is considering. With major bank-related loans the process will involve a specific scrutiny of the lending proposal, the potential customer and the possible collateral of the loan. The kind of modelling outlined above is likely to be part of the process. There are many lending principles which can be applied to these situations. In essence, lending is a specialised decision and where an organisation is providing finance it will need to have the relevant expertise.

In the case of companies which are extending credit there is a similar set of principles based on the nature and size of the transaction. The requirements are in terms of company accounts and bank recommendations.

ESTABLISHING A PORTFOLIO

As indicated by the example of the Texan banks cited above, excessive concentration in threes – having a concentration of exposure to individual customers, sectors, and geographical areas – is to be avoided to ensure that one is not excessively dependent on one's debtors.

The level of credit risks can be reduced if any loans are subject to guarantees. A more recent development in the 1990s are credit derivatives, which are constructed to give pay-offs in adverse credit risk situations. They may pay off all or part of the loss in the event of default. They can be constructed on the basis of amount, recovery rate or maturity, or they may be related to changes in credit rating. Banking institutions may separate their decisions to lend and the concentration of their credit risks.

MANAGING DEBTORS

The more efficiently the debtors are managed, the less likely it is that an organisation will get into serious difficulties over credit risk. It is vital to monitor all contracts where there is an element of credit risk. The early diagnosis and recognition of problems is vital for any sensible credit management. There should also be a policy for creditor treatment.

In recent years banks have offered a number of debtor-related services from extending credit in relation to these types of contract to the management of the debtor relationship.

These debt-factoring services are becoming increasingly common. There are, however, a number of problems with these services for the firms which adopt them. Andy Jesson, a loans officer during his whole career for a number of London-based financial institutions, has always been very critical of using banks for these purposes. He argues that for a business it removes important controls over the business cashflow, and how one deals with debtors is an important element in the customer relationship.

CONCLUSION

In general, the identification and managing of credit risk depends on the type of organisation under consideration. In the case of some organisations, most notably those in the banking industry, managing credit risk is one of the business's core competencies. Banks may spend extensively on systems and staff to ensure each of the credit management processes – from extending the loan, managing the loan, monitoring loans and dealing with bad debt – is done in an efficient and sensible manner. The bank regulator will also be interested in monitoring the adequacy and professionalism of the process. However, it is important that organisations which do not focus on lending as the core competency for their activities should be aware of the credit risks they face and ensure that they are adequately managed.

5

Market risk

INTRODUCTION

Market risks are those related to movements in prices on financial markets. The key sources of risk would relate to interest rates, exchange rates, asset prices, commodity prices and derivatives prices. In association with these risks we will consider those risks associated with the issue of liquidity since it is in analytical terms often associated with the different types of market risk. The management of these risks is often seen as a treasury-based task and this chapter will give an introduction to those treasury-related issues. Although treasury issues are central to this section, there are some issues – for example strategic currency risk – which cannot be seen wholly in treasury terms. The risks relate to the impacts on profitability and in particular shareholder value.

EXAMPLES OF MARKET RISKS

There follows a series of examples of problems for businesses which were the result of movements in financial market prices but which were also associated with operational risk. Frequently these happen because control systems were not adequate and/or because the management did not understand the levels of risk to which the market was subjecting the organisation. Many involved derivatives products which have proven to be difficult to understand and control and in many cases serious, if not terminally damaging. The list of problems is one which is well known – Barings, Metallgesellschaft Corp., Gibson Greetings and National Westminster Bank.

Barings

Nick Leeson, a trader based in Singapore, was responsible in 1995 for destroying Barings bank as an independent entity by speculating on how the Japanese stock market index, the Nikkei, would move in the future. Since he was responsible for both trading and the recording of trades, he was able to hide what was happening from the top management in London. The bank's final losses were in the region of $1.3 billion.

Metallgesellschaft Corp.

One of Germany's largest companies was nearly bankrupted by the activity of a New York-based subsidiary as a result of offering a number of long-term, fixed-price contracts to deliver petroleum-related products from 1992 onwards. These contracts were to some extent hedged, although the hedging – 1–10 year contracts with three-month contracts on the Nymex Futures Market, was unlikely to prove a comprehensive or sensible hedge. In essence, Metallgesellschaft was very heavily exposed to changes in the price of petroleum.

Gibson Greetings Inc. and Bankers Trust Securities Corp.

In 1991, Gibson issued some fixed-interest rate funding with maturities ranging between 1995 and 2001. It became aware of the interest rate risks involved in the funding as interest rates began to fall. Its funding was at interest rates above that current in the market. In order to make its interest rate variable, it entered into an interest rate swap with Bankers Trust – a simple interest rate swap is an exchange of a set of fixed interest rate payments for a set of variable interest rate payments. This deal led to a number of other deals where Gibson entered into further derivative transactions of increasing complication. Since its derivatives were not traded on any market, their valuation could only be made by computer model. Bankers Trust had the valuation models, the skills expertise and software to understand the transactions, but these were not available to Gibson. The market moved against Gibson and overall its losses as valued by Bankers Trust were $16 million, with the revenues generated by Bankers Trust from Gibson at $13 million. The relationship was investigated by the Commodity Futures Trading Commission. Bankers Trust was in the end fined $10 million due to fraudulent misrepresentation and omissions.

National Westminster Bank

In early 1997 National Westminster Bank suspended five members of staff, including two risk managers, and indicated losses on interest rate options of $140 million. The causes of the losses were not entirely clear from NatWest's public statements. A number of possible explanations were suggested for the problems in *Euromoney* of May 1997. It was suggested that the bank had offered the derivatives at values that others in the market found unexpectedly attractive. The motivation for the pricing being not entirely clear, *Euromoney* gave a number of possible explanations: the lack of sophistication of the pricing models used; the lack of realism in the assumptions introduced in the models; the desire for market share; the inability of back and middle offices to stand up to traders who wished to manipulate pricing models. In essence, the valuations of the portfolio were in error and losses were registered.

UK car manufacturing

The euro was established at the beginning of 1999 as a single currency for the majority of members of the European Union. In its first year it fell in value by about one-third relative to sterling. This movement has had a major adverse impact on manufacturing industry in the United Kingdom. In early 2000 the impacts on the motor manufacturing industry were dramatic. BMW, the owner of Rover, reversed its earlier commitment to invest heavily in a plant at Longbridge, near Birmingham, and sold Rover for $15, with a commitment to underwrite further costs within the business. Ford also announced that it was moving car assembly from its plant at Dagenham, in East London, with a loss of 2000 jobs. Nissan, whose plant in Sunderland is the most productive car plant outside Japan, is moving production of some lines to within the euro area. The car manufacturing industry within the UK has proved very sensitive to exchange rate movements at a time of global overcapacity in the automobile industry.

These specific examples are of individual organisations, but all organisations may be subject to certain types of market risks. The most obvious example of this would be in relation to the US stock market collapse in 1929, which precipitated the depression in all the major world economies, which led to the Second World War. In general, financial crises appear to be likely sources of global depressions, although in the 1990s crises in particular financial markets had major impacts on the levels of activity in certain countries. The depression suffered by Japan through most of the 1990s was related to the collapses in the Japanese stock market. The withdrawal of funds from Russia, the Far East and South America precipitated asset market falls and resulted in recessions in these countries during the latter years of the 1990s.

TYPES OF MARKET RISK

The main types of market risk are exchange rate risk, interest rate risk, asset price risk and commodity price risk. There are also risks which depend on the changes in the value of derivative financial obligations and these value changes are dependent on the prime drivers of market risk. In this section we will also deal with liquidity risk.

Exchange rate risk

The risks which businesses face in terms of changes of exchange rates are usually divided into three categories: transactions exposure, translation exposure and economic exposure.

Transactions exposure

Transactions exposure relates to the requirement to pay for a transaction in a foreign currency at a future date which is not matched by any other payments in the foreign currency. There is an uncertainty as to the exchange rate at that particular date.

Translation exposure

Translation exposure is related to accounting for assets, liabilities, or business conducted in a currency different from a business's main domestic currency. The incorporation of the overseas accounts, for example those of a subsidiary, will depend on the technique of consolidation. The results will be based on the value of the exchange rate between currencies. In essence, there will be no change in the cashflow structure of the business, but it may have some serious impacts. Changes in exchange rates may change financial ratios, as in for example gearing and equity cover. These may have impacts to covenants in relation to a firm's debt or the business's banking relationship.

Economic exposure

Economic exposure relates to the risks to organisations which stem from changes in real exchange rates between currencies. Real exchange rates are constant if the change in the exchange rate compensates for any difference between two countries' rates of inflation. If the US rate of inflation is 3 per cent and that within the euro area is 4 per cent, then the real exchange rate will remain constant if the dollar rises by 1 per cent in value relative to the euro. This will mean that if a car is produced in the US and can be sold for $20 000, at the end of the year it will be sold for $20 600. Abstracting from transport costs, if $1 = 1 euro, then the price in the euro area at the beginning of the year will be 20 000 euros. At the end of the year it will be 20 800 euros. If a comparable car produced within the euro area is initially sold for 20 000 euros, at the end of the year it will also be priced, given domestic inflation, at 20 800 euros. If currency values move in relation to inflation, no economic advantage is obtained by either country. If the real exchange rate changes and currency values do not just reflect relative inflation, there may be major business risks. The example in relation to the UK car industry reflects the fact that over 1999/2000 the real euro-to-pound exchange rate did not purely reflect rates of inflation.

Interest rate risk

Interest rate risk is related to risks for the profitability and value for a business which are determined by changes in interest rates. There is a diversity of interest rates in any given economy and risks may be associated with the levels of rates or the relationships between the different rates. The most obvious example of how interest rates work can be seen in the savings and loans crisis in the US which has been referred to previously. The savings and loans or thrifts – or to use the term for these institutions in the UK, South Africa and Australia, building societies – in the US raised funds short term with variable interest rates and lent long at fixed interest rates. When interest rates rose, the funding became more expensive while the interest revenues did not change. In essence, interest rate risk is related to the timing of repricing in relation to borrowing and lending.

Asset price risk

There are many risks related to the prices of financial assets. They may be caused by changes in exchange rates and interest rates since if these change they will impact on the prices of different assets. Asset pricing theories, in the main, work on the basis of predicting the cashflows associated with the asset and applying an interest rate to those cashflows. If interest rates fall, one would expect the value of equities and debt vehicles to rise.

Commodity price risks

Changes in the levels of commodity prices can have a major impact on some businesses where these are a major input or have an impact on the demand for the business of the enterprise. The price of petrol can be seen over the past few decades to have an extensive impact on a number of different businesses, including oil companies, transport enterprises, power companies, car manufacturers and so on.

Liquidity risk

Liquidity risk relates to the ease with which a particular set of financial obligations can be sold in the marketplace. The degree of risk depends on the levels of market turnover. The greater the market turnover, the lower the fees for the market transaction and the greater the liquidity. Markets with high turnover are in general highly liquid, as for example the foreign exchange markets, which trade $1.6 trillion per day. In general, the greater the value of the position to be sold and the shorter the time envisaged for the transaction, the less the liquidity. The liquidity of markets varies markedly and many derivative transactions may be highly illiquid, most notably in the over-the-counter markets. One of the problems for many derivatives is that there is no market price, so pricing depends on mathematical modelling and closing out an obligation depends on another institution being prepared to operate in the market. There are normal levels of liquidity risk, but these may seriously underestimate the problems of liquidation of a position during a financial crisis.

There were serious market liquidity problems during the October 1987 financial crisis and the European Monetary Mechanism crisis of 1992 when the pound exited the ERM. The collapse of Long Term Capital Management (LTCM) in 1998 led to worries for the world financial system. LTCM was a highly leveraged firm, having \$5 billion equity, \$125 billion assets and \$1.25 trillion in face value of derivatives positions (the face value of a derivatives position is the value of the underlying obligation to be bought or sold). The company argued that its risks were limited to those common for most equities and performed trades based on optimisation techniques with a certain level of value at risk. Its problems resulted from its size and the resulting lack of liquidity in the markets when it wished to liquidate problem positions.

Financial derivatives

John C. Hull, in his book *Options, Futures and Other Derivative Securities* (2000, Prentice Hall, fourth edn), defines derivatives in the following terms: 'A derivative is a financial instrument whose value depends on the values of other more basic underlying variables.' Derivatives by their nature are neither risky nor safe, but there have been a large number of major problems for businesses as a result of trading in derivatives. They are not necessarily dangerous, but they can be very dangerous.

However, if one considers many of the examples in relation to derivative prices cited above – for example Barings, Metallgesellschaft and Gibson Greetings – many of the mistakes that underlay the problems were related to problems that were intrinsically simple in retrospect. Buyers and sellers who trade in derivative markets are often categorised in terms of hedgers who wish to offset other risks in their business by entering the derivatives markets, arbitrageurs who wish to make money by exploiting any anomalies in these markets, and speculators who use these instruments to undertake risks. It is important, if trading in these markets, to ensure the organisation understands the intrinsic risks.

As we outlined earlier, a number of the standard derivative products are traded on financial markets such as the Chicago Board of Trade, the Philadelphia Stock Exchange and the London International Futures and Options Exchange. Many other derivatives are traded in essence between financial institutions and corporates on an individual basis in what are called the over-the-counter markets. There may be some liquidity risk with the market-based derivatives, but there is usually a market price for particular quoted obligations. With OTC derivatives they may be individually crafted and there are no necessary market prices for these obligations. Their valuation may therefore be possible only with very elaborate financial models. The pricing of a type of obligation called an option – which is essentially a right to buy or sell – may require very sophisticated mathematics, and as the National Westminster Bank example quoted above indicates, it is possible for different institutions to disagree about the valuation of these options.

Given the widespread issues in relation to the risk which can be created by derivatives it is important for senior management to have an idea of how they work and what systems should be in place to sensibly deal with their risks. There are too many examples of organisations that believed they had hedged their risks by derivatives only to find that not only were their risks not hedged but that they had taken risks they had not even imagined. What follows is a simple introduction to the nature of derivatives. The different types of derivative can be combined to form more exotic derivatives such as swaptions, a combination of a swap and an option.

Forwards and futures

Forwards and futures are agreements to deliver an obligation at a fixed price at some agreed date in the future. There are many differences between the two types of contracts futures being traded on exchanges and forwards being traded in OTC markets. Initially these contracts were for commodities such as wheat, so the farmer for example could guarantee a price for his crops in advance. However, these contracts are now extended to diverse financial obligations. Some of the more common forward and futures contracts relate to commodities, interest rates, exchange rates, share prices and market indices.

Swaps

Swaps are traded on the OTC markets and are agreements to exchange cashflows between parties. The cashflows are based on certain interest rates. There are two major types of swap: interest rate swaps and foreign exchange swaps. With an interest rate swap in a particular currency one party may agree to pay a fixed rate, for example 5.34 per cent, and receive from the other party a rate based on a variable rate, for example three-hundreds of a percent below the three-month Libor, which is a market interest rate. An example of why a party might enter into this arrangement would be if a UK building society lent money at a variable interest rate and wished to fund it with fixed interest rate funding. It would raise the fixed-interest rate funding and swap variable payments for receiving fixed payments, which it would use to pay the interest on the fixed-rate funding. An exchange rate swap involves the exchange of cashflows in different currencies at rates related to interest rates in the two currencies chosen.

Options

An option is an obligation to buy or sell at a particular price. The seller of the option agrees to buy or sell at a particular price while the buyer does not have to take up the offer and is expected only to take it up if it is in their interests to do so. Options are traded on both markets and OTC. They are traded in relation to a number of obligations, including commodities, shares, interest rates, exchange rates and market indices.

Valuation of derivatives

The valuation of derivatives is an abstruse and arcane activity of which the most basic principle can only be indicated. There are many risks which derive from pricing derivatives since in the case of complicated derivative products they can be priced only in terms of institutions coming to an agreed price in the OTC market or estimated on the basis of mathematical models. The most basic ideas for the different types of derivatives are outlined in what follows.

Forwards and futures

The relationship between the market price of, say, a quantity of wheat and its forward/futures price is determined by the following hypothetical transactions. A buyer can buy now and store for the price of K + S, where K is the current price of the wheat and S represents the storage cost. They could agree now the forward wheat contract for F and invest the money to get a return of R, the total price being F + R. Since these two transactions have exactly the same impact, the market will ensure that they are equally priced, so the pricing formula for the option is $F = K + S - R$. Having agreed the contract, the F is fixed immutably, but the price of wheat for current purchase can vary. If it falls, buying wheat by the futures contract has been a bad investment, while if it rises, the futures contract has been a good investment. The value of the futures contract initially is in this sense zero but through time it will vary, representing gains and losses to the parties to the forward/futures contract.

Swaps

The valuation of a swap is the valuation of the two cashflows. In the initial contract the parties will enter into it only if the value of the contract is zero. In other words the value of the two cashflows is the same. After the contract is established, interest rates will change – for example, if rates rise and you are paying fixed and receiving floating interest rates, you will gain because your payments will not change but you will receive more.

Options

Options valuation can be very complicated. In recent years it has attracted the attention of many applied mathematicians. The most famous option pricing model was that of Black and Scholes and involved the application of mathematics used in engineering to finance. The individuals who build option-pricing software are likely to be PhDs in mathematics from top universities. Thus what follows is a very simplistic story about options pricing and focuses only on the factors which are likely to influence a simple options price. If we consider the option to be the ability but not the obligation to buy a share in British Telecom in July for 995, the current price of the share in May being 992, what factors are likely to influence the value of this option? The standard option-pricing theory would suggest the factors outlined in Table 5.1.

Table 5.1 Factors which determine options value – example of a call

Strike price	The price at which the option can be exercised, in this case 995. The higher this price, the lower the value of the option since one is less likely to be able to buy the share and sell it at a profit.
Current price	The current price of 992 if it were to be the price up to the end of the period when the option can be exercised would mean the option would never be profitable to exercise. However, the share price varies through time and the higher the price, the greater the probability that it will rise to a price to make exercise profitable. The higher the current price, the more valuable the option.
Rate of interest	If the share price is high relative to the exercise price of the option, then buying the option is equivalent to buying the share today but paying at expiry. One might invest the value of the exercise price and invest the interest. The possibility of that transaction is incorporated in the exercise price, so the option price rises with the interest rate.
Volatility	The more volatile the share price, the more likely that the share will rise to a level to make the option profitable, so the value of the option rises with the volatility of the share price.
Remaining time	The longer the time to the expiry of the option, the more likely the share price will rise to levels which make the option profitable, therefore the more valuable the option is.

COMMONLY OCCURRING OPTIONS FOR BUSINESSES

There are a number of options which are faced by businesses which do not deal in standard derivative products. The two main categories are in the way funds are raised for a business and/or real options which often relate to investment opportunities.

In raising funding for the public companies there has been an increasing use of financial instruments which have options included in their construction. Examples of these vehicles would include warrants, convertibles and asset-backed securities. Warrants are rights to buy a company's shares, convertibles are bonds which may be converted into shares, and asset-backed securities are fund-raising instruments which provide investors with cashflows based on an underlying asset's cashflows. The most common example of this relates to mortgage-backed assets where the buyer of the security receives a share of the interest and capital payments of a portfolio of mortgages. The optionality relates to the fact that mortgage customers have the option to pay off or pre-pay their mortgages.

The other major issue concerning real options is that many investment projects have as part of their rationale an option embedded in the project. The valuation of these options can be undertaken with the tools developed for financial options pricing. The more standard types of investment projects are as follows. The inclusion of real options in this section is due simply to the convenience in explaining them in the same section as financial options. They tend to relate to operational rather than market risk.

If an investment is made it will provide the possibility of choosing to make follow-on investments which would not be the case if the investment were not made. The decision as to whether to make the follow-up investment will depend on future circumstances. The motivation for many businesses entering the e-commerce distribution channel is not limited short-run financial benefits but the knowledge and branding which may not be available to the firm with later entry into this market, which may become the retailing channel in the future.

Consider a situation in which a business has a choice of investment in plant which is sufficiently specific that it has no secondhand sale value if the project is not a success or plant which has a secondhand value. The first set of plant is purpose-built and thus has lower costs. The comparison should take into account the fact that if business is poor, one of the choices has an option in relation to withdrawal costs.

Another type of option is related to a project that is risky and may provide a high level of return or a poor return dependent on circumstances. If over time one can obtain a better view of circumstance, there may be an option in relation to when the investment should be made. It is in fact an issue as to when or whether an option should be exercised.

A further type of real option relates to the introduction of flexibility into the commercial process. This also represents an option which can be exercised given the specific circumstances. Toyota, for example, has a number of production facilities in different countries and its decisions about production in a particular location will be dependent in part on exchange rates. A rise in the yen-dollar exchange rate in the early 1990s led to an increase in exports of the Camry from US plants to Japan.

If one considers these examples of common business options, the ones in relation to funding are likely to be sensibly priced and handled since the issue of these obligations is likely to be undertaken with the correct levels of professional advice. The case with real options is less clear. My experience is that many businesses and public companies do not adequately consider the issue of optionality in relation to their business decisions. It should, though infrequently is, an issue which will be dealt with as part of the capital appraisal proposals.

MANAGING MARKET RISKS

As with all risk management systems the type of system that an organisation sets up will depend on its size and attitude to risk. As a general proposition in this book it will be the case that we will consider how a large business with substantial resources would manage risks. To articulate best practice will enable smaller organisations to understand what they require and make judgements as to what they can afford. The practical issues will be dealt with in the next section of the book; in this section we will consider the theoretical issues.

The explanation of how to hedge market risks is often defined in terms of the hedging of a particular risk. Increasingly, organisations see hedging in terms of aggregating the risks of an organisation and hedging any exposures which are evident from an analysis of the portfolio. To be able to conduct the analysis necessary to undertake this overall hedging for financial risks involves sophisticated information systems, staff and analytical tools.

We have considered, for example, looking at risk in terms of Monte Carlo simulations and the calculation of value at risk. These would represent two ways of analysing risks which would allow the organisation to consider the financial risks it wished to hedge with the various types of financial instrument.

CONCLUSION

Market risks impact on all organisations. They impact partly through the firm's financial obligations but also in relation to the general level of its operations. Exchange rates and interest rates have major impacts on most firms. Care should be taken when a firm has a derivatives exposure since there are many examples of businesses encountering major problems in relation to their derivatives holdings.

Section 3

A practical risk management system

6

Establishing a risk management system

INTRODUCTION

Looking at the diverse examples in the previous chapters it is obvious that many disasters can hit businesses which could have been avoided if a sensible risk management policy had been in place. A sensible risk management policy will never be able to guarantee the immortality of an organisation, but it will be able to make some mistakes less likely, and the adverse impacts of these events less serious. There is thus in general terms a strong case for the implementation of risk management systems.

There are also developments in terms of the regulatory environment for certain organisations, which would give an extra impetus for the establishing of a comprehensive firm-wide risk management system. The banking systems of all developed countries have become more regulated in terms of risk management. The core impetus for this has been the Bank of International Settlements, whose regulations have been adopted by bank regulators in all the major world economies. There are moves to develop standards for non-financial businesses, for example in relation to the Turnbull working party of the Institute of Chartered Accountants of England and Wales. It has published 'Guidance for directors of listed companies incorporated in the United Kingdom'. There is also development of standards in Canada, Australia and New Zealand. Having an effective risk management system will become a necessary attribute of any well-managed company, and it may become part of the requirement for companies listed on major stock markets. There are also many other risk-related laws and regulations to which any organisation may be subject, for example in relation to health and safety, and labour legislation. Some industries have specific safety issues which require specialised risk management systems.

Having determined the necessity for a general risk management system we will consider the ways to establish one. The key component of the process involves the steps listed in Figure 6.1. These should not be seen as listed in chronological order for establishing a comprehensive risk management system but rather as the components of an organisational system that will work effectively. Each of these categories is introduced here but forms the material to be considered in subsequent chapters.

ATTITUDE TO RISK

Any organisation that seeks to establish a comprehensive risk management system must ask a number of questions about its attitudes to risk. It will be subject to some risk whether it has a comprehensive risk management system or not, so it needs to consider which risks it wishes to take and on what terms. If one considers commercial businesses, they will have a number of stakeholders and part of risk management is to decide in whose interests we are undertaking risk management. The attitudes of shareholders, managers, customers, workers, and bondholders may be different in relation to the different types of risk. To take an obvious example which we will consider in detail in a later chapter, managers' and shareholders' interests are not necessarily congruent. Shareholders are likely to diversify their risks by investing in a number of businesses but management is likely to be less able to diversify the sources of their income and wealth. Therefore managers are likely to be more risk averse than shareholders.

Fig. 6.1 **Elements of a risk management system**

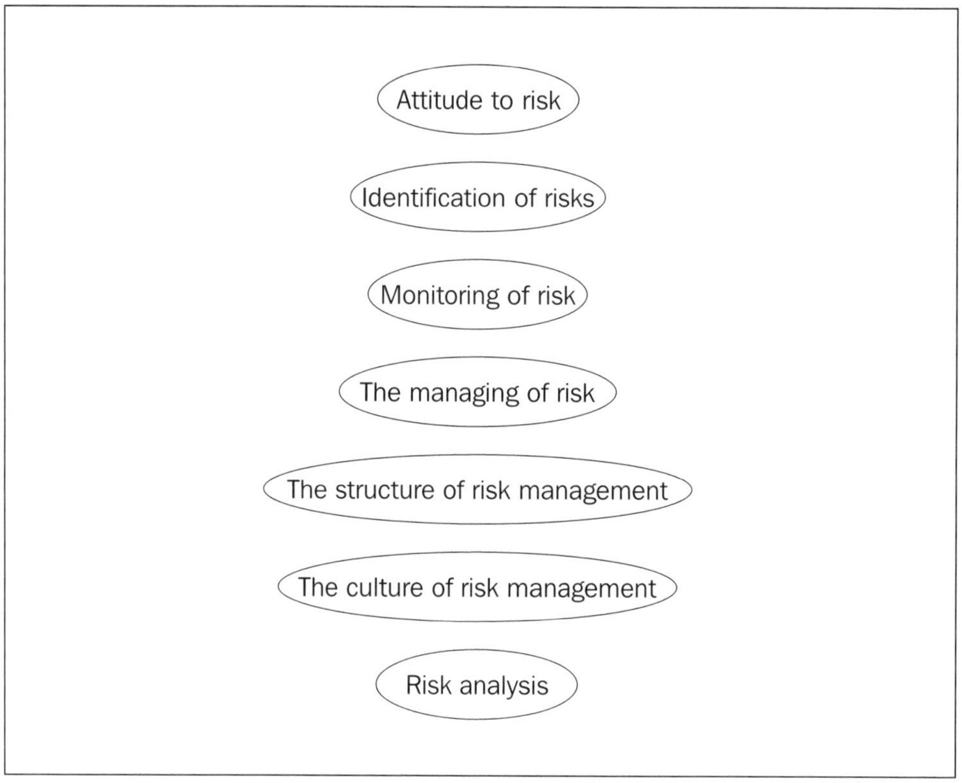

IDENTIFICATION OF RISKS

A prelude to the establishing of any risk management system is to identify as accurately as possible risks which an organisation faces. This will never be a totally comprehensive process but it will need to try to be as comprehensive as possible. Having identified risks at one point in time it is important to replicate this process at regular intervals. It may be sensible to update the process on at least an annual basis since the risks faced by the organisation will change and sometimes a new process leads to the identification of extra risks which had previously not been considered. Having identified possible risks it is important to then consider in detail how each is to be managed, and that is part of the process for defining what exactly is the organisation's attitude to risk.

MONITORING RISK

Risk identification should lead to an ongoing monitoring of the risks identified. This may involve a major systems development process. But if risks are to be effectively managed it is important to be able to monitor the degree to which they change in relation to the organisation. It is important to note that not all risks need necessarily to be monitored. There are some which will be too unimportant to consider, and others for which monitoring really is not an essential part of their management. To give an example of this type of risk, most financial institutions are worried that a jumbo jet may fall on their computer centre, so they have a back-up centre. As long as the back-up is operational they do not need to consider the changing probability that a jumbo will crash on their computer centre.

RISK ANALYSIS

To understand the risks to which an organisation is subject it is important to have some analytical facility in relation to risk. Analytical techniques have been discussed in relation to market and credit risks but it may also be important to subject some operational risks to analysis. The system, if it is comprehensive, will not necessarily be integrated since it will require the ability to undertake a diversity of ad hoc as well as regular analysis.

THE MANAGEMENT OF RISK

Having identified the risks and decided how they will be dealt, with it is important to put in place whatever mechanisms are required for the management of the risk. If, for example, there is a need to establish disaster recovery plans, these should be established and the processes they recommend put in place, including the facility for their updating at regular intervals. There is an increasing emphasis on managing certain types of operational risks by instituting appropriate control of processes.

The structure of risk management

One of the major lessons with risk management is that when risks are identified and a policy put in place for dealing with them, managerial responsibility should be allocated to particular individuals. This will ensure that the policies identified are specifically implemented. However, the task may be far from easy given the diversity of risks which an organisation may face.

The culture of risk management

If an enterprise is to have a comprehensive risk management system it is important that all staff should be involved in the risk management process. There is also an important issue in relation to the reporting of certain risk-related problems. Some of the examples cited previously became worse because the risks involved were not made public within the organisations. This factor was an aspect of problems for Gibsons' Greetings, Metallgesellschaft, and a number of the bank failures. An open culture will provide information that may prove vital in the understanding of risks. The airline industry has an open culture for reporting problems and near-misses. This type of culture may prove a useful adjunct of any sensible risk management within an organisation.

CONCLUSION

There is increasing pressure for well-managed firms to establish general systems of risk management. This pressure is coming from regulators and the accountancy profession in a number of countries. In general terms, a review of what has happened to a number of organisations illustrates the many problems that ostensibly well-managed businesses have faced which would not have arisen if they had had a sensible risk management system in place.

7

Attitudes to risk

INTRODUCTION

This chapter will consider the attitudes to risk that should underpin an organisation-wide risk management system. It will focus initially on the issue of whose attitudes to risk should dominate the risk management policy and then look at the issue of what levels of return a business should require in relation to the risks which it undertakes. These two issues are in fact strongly related because the different stakeholders may have different attitudes to the problem of risk-adjusted returns.

ATTITUDE TO RISK: A CONFLICT OF INTEREST

Any organisation has a number of stakeholders. For a business, the main ones are likely to be the shareholders, managers, workers, customers, suppliers, regulators and debt holders. Each of these has a different attitude and set of interests in relation to the organisation. All are subject to or interested in the risks which relate to the organisation. In general, the stakeholders which have primacy in establishing a risk management policy will be the managers and shareholders. The other stakeholders, although important to the development of a risk management policy, will be seen rather as subjects, whose risks should be managed if the business is to be effective, than as key elements in forming policy. There is also an issue as to whether the managers of a business on occasions set up a risk management system so that it benefits their interests rather than that of the shareholders. It is my view that this is often the case and if firms embrace the shareholder value principle they should reflect this in their risk management policies.

THE BENEFITS OF RISK MANAGEMENT

The difference between a shareholder's view of risk management and that of the management can be understood in terms of the degree of diversification the two groups have in relation to the risks of the business. Sensible shareholders will diversify their risks and hold shares in a number of businesses. This is the case with most holders of shares. The individual who holds shares in one or two companies is the rarity. Most holders of shares are institutional shareholders, all of which will be heavily diversified. Behind many of these institutions are a large proportion of the population who own shares through institutional investors such as pension funds and unit trusts.

Shareholders are diversified. Managers on the other hand are likely to be less diversified. Their income will be heavily dependent on the jobs that they hold. Their pension funds will be associated with the company they work for and although independent may to some extent be related to the performance of the business. The motivational structure of most corporates ensures that managers have shares and options on the shares in the companies for which they work. Although there are ways of spreading the risks these managers face, generally, they do not diversify their risks. There is some evidence from the US that company executives enter financial markets to diversify their risks by the purchase of options in the firms they work in. If managers indulge in this activity it runs counter to the principles on which they are remunerated which are to motivate them by making their income and wealth related to the performance of the business.

The argument which follows from this distinction is that risk can be divided into two categories, one called specific risk and the other called market risk. Specific risks relate to the individual circumstance of a particular company, while market risk relates to the risks of a diversified portfolio. Investors are not interested in specific risks since they will be diversified by holding a portfolio of assets, they are interested in how risky a share is in terms of the risks they cannot diversify, which are called market risks. They relate to how a share return will vary in relation to risks that cannot be diversified. The required returns to shareholders relate to these kinds of risk and the capital asset pricing model and the arbitrage pricing model are attempts to measure these risks and formulate what would be an adequate return in relation to these risks.

Thus there is a proposition that shareholders are not interested in businesses which hedge certain kinds of risks. They may also wish to buy shares with different levels of risk to accommodate their taste and hedging policy. The traditional argument about risk has been that risk management policy may improve the value of the firm in the following ways. If a company is subject to variable cashflows the probability of financial distress will be increased so the value of the business will be decreased. A company with more predictable, stable cashflows may find internal funding easier to create and thus avoid recourse to external funding markets which are more expensive. More stability of cashflows may also have tax benefits and so enhance the value of the firm.

The implication of these arguments is that risk management policies reduce the variability of cashflows or profitability. In fact, many risk management policies do more than that – they can also raise the returns in relation to the business as well as reducing risk. If we consider many of the examples of business risks encountered above they may lead to higher returns for the business by eliminating high downside risks. The key idea can be seen in Figure 7.1. An individual risk management project can add value for a business by lowering the variability of cashflows in order to have less risk in terms of those risks which the shareholder values or in terms of increasing the average return. The initiatives which are undertaken should be those which satisfy the condition that the value they create in revenue terms should exceed the value of the costs. This approach can be summarised in the following terms: that any risk management initiative is in essence the same as any other use of the firm's funding and should be justified in those terms. It should be subject to the same criteria as, for example, capital investment.

Fig. 7.1 Risk management policies that raise value

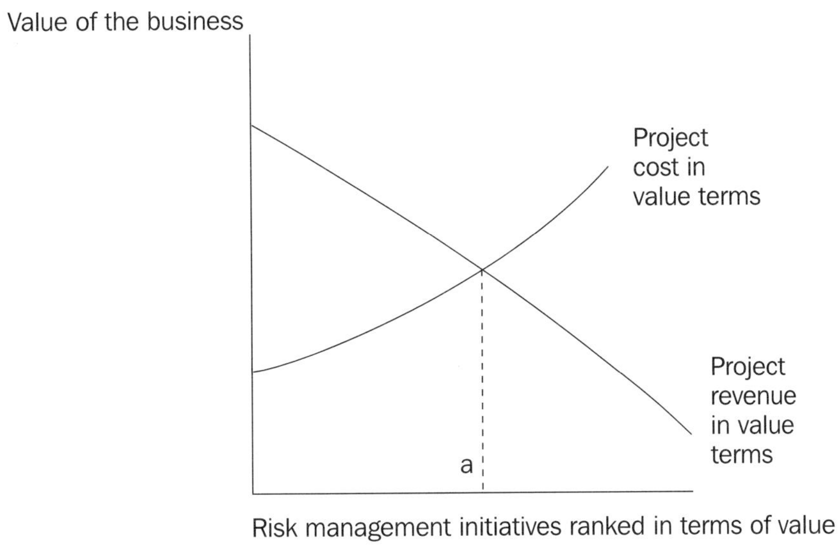

WHAT IS THE REQUIRED RETURN TO SHAREHOLDERS?

Increasingly, businesses and investors are asking the question, how much return is merited in relation to a particular degree of risk? We can evaluate returns only in relation to the risks with which they are associated. There are numerous measures and any decision to use them within a particular business situation will require a specialised understanding of their nature. This section merely provides an overview of what they are and how they can be evaluated. In general they relate a measure of return to a measure of risk. The measure of return is invariably the average or expected level of return for a particular time period.

The level of risk can be measured in a number of ways. There are three common measures of risk which we met in the introductory chapters – the standard deviation or variance of the return, the value at risk, or the worst case. These measures can be applied to a business or any unit within a business such as a decision, a product, a capital expenditure. There are also other measures of risk which come from the finance theory in relation to the risks which shareholders cannot hedge without cost. Most large business enterprises have used the CAPM (capital asset pricing model) to decide what is the appropriate return for a given level of risk. This measure of risk has been subject to much criticism and most finance specialists have more confidence in arbitrage pricing theory but this has not been popular with businesses because it is difficult to implement since it requires a higher level of technical statistical competence than does the CAPM.

The core problem with risk management is that there is no single, generally accepted view as to what forms an appropriate return in relation to risk. Finance theory has in the past operated on the principle that the required return for a certain level of risk should be that required on the capital markets. However, the finance industry, following the lead of Bankers Trust, has taken a different approach based on the role of capital as a buffer against organisational bankruptcy. The two approaches can be summarised in the following terms.

The traditional finance view of required returns can be expressed in terms of Equation 7.1. The required return for taking a certain level of risk for activity i is **Ri** which can be calculated in terms of two components – a risk-free component **Rf**, usually measured by the rates on the appropriate term of government debt, and a return which reflects a premia for the specific risk of the employment of funds **Rri**. The main problem is in the calculation of **Rri**. The CAPM estimates it in terms of Equation 7.2, where the risk premia is calculated in terms of the difference between the market rate of return and the risk-free rate multiplied by the level of risk to be awarded which is measured by **βi**. The calculation of **βi** is simply a measure of the degree to which returns in this activity vary with returns in the asset market generally. The individual enterprises which need to decide on the level of βi will find that there are βs calculated for all the major firms which are readily available.

Equation 7.1

$$\mathbf{Ri = Rf + Rri}$$

Equation 7.2

$$\mathbf{Rri = \beta i(Rm - Rf)}$$

When considering the activities of individual elements of a business it is important to choose the right level of risk and this is in many ways an art form rather than a science and needs to be undertaken by trained finance staff. Having determined the level of return required on an activity it will then be necessary to determine what funds are required in the activity and this is simply the negative cashflows of the project. The technique in deciding if an activity is worthwhile is to identify the positive and negative cashflows and the time periods in which they occur and discount them with the required rate of return. If the result is positive, the activity is worth the risk; if that is not the case, the activity is not worth the risk. It should be added that there may be options associated with these calculations and they should be considered on the basis of the relevant option-pricing valuation.

In recent years a number of financial organisations and consultancies – notably Bankers Trust and Price Waterhouse (before its merger with Coopers and Lybrand) – developed a different view of the appropriate returns to risk within the finance industry. The initial context of the development was the view that capital is a buffer against the bankruptcy of a business and banking supervision has suggested that certain levels of business require certain levels of capital to ensure the likely solvency of the banking institution. The regulations led to banks allocating capital to particular activities, initially on the basis of regulators' estimates and later on the basis of internal risk models. The procedure, which has come to be recognised as best practice in the banking industry, is to allocate capital on the basis of value at risk. The capital is allocated so that the activity will be insufficient only in the very severest of crises. Having allocated capital on this basis, the returns of the activity are divided by the capital at risk to obtain a measure termed return on risk adjusted capital or Rorac. The higher Rorac, the more desirable the activity.

To decide whether a given level of Rorac is acceptable one sets targets for the required levels of profitability for the organisation. This technique has a number of problems which make it undesirable as a method for establishing a required return to risk. The capital allocated is invariably not the same as that required by the regulators. It does not reflect any external market views on the returns of the activities in question, a riskless investment will always have an infinite Rorac since it requires no capital. There are many weaknesses with the technique but suffice to note that if one has to choose between it and the CAPM technique, at least the CAPM has some sensible market and finance justification.

CONCLUSION

In considering the setting up of a risk management system for a business where the objective of the business is to maximise shareholder value it is vital to ensure that the risks which are managed are those which the shareholder wishes to manage. If managing risk increases the value of the business by enhancing the average return of the business or reduces the variability of the returns that shareholders are interested in, then it is valuable. If it reduces risks at cost and those risks are already diversified by the shareholder's portfolio, then it is not desirable. In considering what is an appropriate return to risk there are many choices, none of which is entirely satisfactory, but probably the most sensible from a shareholder's perspective are those related to the CAPM.

8

The identification of risks

INTRODUCTION

In order to establish an enterprise-wide risk management system it is necessary to identify the risks which a business faces. This may prove difficult given the diversity of risks. It should not be seen as an exercise that is ever complete or comprehensive since it is impossible to identify all the risks that an organisation is facing and given the perpetual change of activities in large businesses, the risks will be changing all the time. However, it is an important exercise to undertake since the identification of risks is one of the first major steps in managing risk. One must also indicate that a sensible risk management system will be able to provide some protection for the risks that are not necessarily identified, since for example if one can identify what is at risk in an organisation it is possible provide contingency plans in relation to those resources.

THE DIFFERENT TYPES OF RISK

We have categorised risks into market risks, credit risks and operational risks. The identification and management of many market risks is in essence a treasury-based operation and the specialists needed to manage these types of risks if they are important to a company are those with extensive treasury risk management backgrounds. With credit risks again there are specialist disciplines which need to be applied for credit management. There are thus specialist skills relating to many different types of risk.

Table 8.1 identifies some of the skills which can be deployed in relation to aspects of risk management. It is important in the identification and management of risks to draw on the particular skills required for the precise nature of one's activities. If an organisation does not process the relevant skills it may wish to draw on outside skills through the use of consultants or through recruitment. Certainly in the risk identification process there is a strong argument for drawing on the experience of other organisations.

Relying exclusively on the internal experience of an organisation is in principle very dangerous as groups generally tend to be rather blinkered to the nature of the risks that they face. It is useful in the identification of risks to have an outside reality check, particularly from individuals or organisations which have seen the risks faced by similar organisations. There is lots of outside knowledge and experience for all businesses and it is important to learn from it.

The most difficult exercise in risk identification is in relation to operational risks. Many of these risks are specialised and therefore the relevant specialist skills should be drawn on. Most organisations face a diversity of legal-based risks and these can be properly addressed only by adequately skilled legal staff. There is a tendency often for businesses to employ less able legal staff since the best continue in private practice, so one should ensure that where internal legal staff are insufficiently skilled their analysis is augmented by outside legal skills. To take an example from my own experience, my wife is a lawyer and she had a case in relation to a mortgage fraud where there were problems as to whether the bank had made a valid contract with the alleged fraudster. The argument undermined the way UK banks set up their mortgage contracts in many instances. The point eventually went to the highest court in the UK, the House of Lords, and the judgement went against the bank's vision of the contract. At that time I was working for a bank and when I suggested to the legal department that this might prove a major problem they ignored it. Having a legal department does not guarantee sensible legal advice.

Table 8.1 **Risk management disciplines**

Market risk	Treasury risk management
Credit risk	Credit management
Operational risk	Health and safety IT risk Engineering safety evaluation Quality control Contingency planning The law Hazard engineering Hazard identification procedures – Hazop (Hazard and Operability Study), Hazan (Hazard Analysis)

Identifying operational risks may prove difficult and one should look for aids to ensuring a wide scanning for possible risks. Chapter 3 on operational risks may provide some categories but it is important to draw the net as wide as possible.

THE PROCESS OF RISK IDENTIFICATION

In setting up an organisation-wide risk management system it is essential to establish the potential risks facing the organisation. This will initially require the setting up of a risk identification project. The project must draw on outside experience if it is to be successful, since both an internal and an external perspective will ensure that a wider range of risks are identified. It is also important not to draw the team from one particular environment within the organisation or with one particular set of skills. These projects may initially be related or managed by the finance or auditing function but it would be a big mistake to staff the project team with only finance specialists. A finance background will not make you particularly alert to many business and operational risks. It is also useful if the team is drawn widely from the organisation for developing and exploiting contacts and bringing wider credibility to the project.

There is some debate about whether the process of risk identification should be handled by a team centrally or should draw widely on the experience of individuals in the operating units. When Bankers Trust set up its risk management system it used a centrally based investigation team using information from within and outside the bank. I have worked with other banks which have used organisational workshops for the identification and evaluation of their risks. The choice between the two methods depends in part on the degree to which an organisation wants to embed a risk management culture within the whole organisation. A process of workshops and drawing operating units into the management of their risks means that the process will reflect the detail and knowledge embedded in the organisation. It will also make the operating units aware of how they fit into the organisational system of risk management.

THE CAUSES AND EFFECTS OF RISK

The most sensible and practical way to identify risks is to consider them from two perspectives – cause and effect. This is the perspective outlined in terms of development with the US military and the Institute of Chartered Accountants of England and Wales to identify what is at risk in an organisation and how it is at risk. This method has already been presented in general terms but in this section it is explored in more detail and is presented in a form based on a number of modifications which I have made to the process.

The dual perspective is important because it provides an extensive brainstorming tool when used in detail, as illustrated in this chapter. It also allows us to focus on what is at risk without always being aware of how it is at risk. The Chicago Board of Trade might not have been aware of the problems with flooding (*see* p. 11) but it had considered what it would do in terms of contingency planning if its IT and telecommunications became ineffective. The dual perspective gives clues as to where the risks might lie proves a useful tool either within the risk identification team or with workshops within the organisation.

In developing the analysis in relation to businesses it is important to understand that there is an element of fuzziness about the techniques. When we consider the categories of resource of the business we will, for example, look at issues concerning reputation and customers. These two categories are not entirely unrelated but it helps to keep them separate to aid in the provision of as wide a perspective as possible for the risk identification process. There is also some fuzziness as a result of the fact that some of the categories of causes and effects are the same; for example, people may be a vital resource of an organisation but also a source of problems for the organisation. The process of this analytical tool is to help identify risks; the fact that it has some logical fuzziness is not an important issue with regard to its purpose.

WHAT IS AT RISK?

The identification of the resources of a business is becoming more complicated as firms and economies become more sophisticated. The key business resource in the 19th century was capital, but now that capital is relatively plentiful the key business resources are increasingly becoming intangibles.

As a start to the process of identification of risks a strategic review of the organisation tends to be useful in establishing what is key for the business's success. There are a number of consultants who suggest that a key risk identification process is to subject the business to a value chain analysis, the purpose of which is to identify the key links in the value chain and where the organisation creates most value. This should indicate the areas of the organisation on which any risk analysis should focus. Irrespective of the specific tools of strategic analysis, an understanding of the key ways in which a businesses intends to generate value, both currently and in the future, is a good precursor to any sensible risk identification exercise.

Considering the assets of a business which are at risk, the following analysis suggests a useful set of categories with which to start: physical assets, financial obligations, inputs, performance, outputs, suppliers and associated business relationships, customers, people, information systems, processes, operational systems, culture, and reputation. Increasingly, if businesses are to establish high levels of return the key assets are the ones listed at the end rather than at the beginning of the list. If one considers why many consultancy businesses, for example, yield high levels of return it is not because of the premises, computers or fixed assets generally but because of the quality of staff, the contacts in the customer business community and the methodologies in the consultancy activities which they undertake. We will consider each of the resource categories in turn.

Physical assets

The key physical assets of any business are likely to be the premises, IT and communications assets. These assets of a business may not be the key to the delivering of shareholder value but often if a business is deprived of them, then the business will find it impossible to function. Robin Kendall in his book on risk management (Risk Management for Executives, 1998, Pitman) cites the example that nearly 50 per cent of the businesses in the World Trade Centre when it was blown up were subsequently to go bankrupt. One of the major aspects of contingency planning is to consider how the business would continue if something happened to its physical assets. Therefore it is vital to consider the risks to the physical assets of the business.

Financial obligations

The financial obligations of a business can be a key source of value. Market risk and credit risk relate directly to the financial assets and liabilities of a business. One should see the management of these risks in part in terms of market and credit risk management. It is important when addressing the funding of risks to consider the possibilities of risk in relation to the perceived creditworthiness of the organisation being lowered. A large corporate may face increased funding costs if, for example, its credit rating falls.

Inputs

The quality of inputs of a business is often a key determinant in its success. If one considers the ability of restaurants to produce high quality food this will depend in part on high quality ingredients. A continuity of supply of appropriate ingredients is thus a pre-requisite for the success of the restaurant. There are many businesses which depend for their success on their ability to obtain a continuous supply of inputs.

Performance

All risks are related to a business performance and if a risk impacts on one of the other asset categories it will impact on the organisational performance. However, there are causes of risk which may not operate on anything other than the firm's performance. For example, if there is a fall in the demand for a firm's products it will only indirectly impact on the other assets of the business, but it may seriously undermine profitability and shareholder value. The problems in the UK manufacturing industry as a result of the relative overvaluation of the pound to the euro have impacted on performance rather than on the other assets.

Outputs

Products and services of a business are a central vital basis for its success since they are what it sells and what generates revenue. Problems with product quality can be related to reputational issues and quality problems can have a long-term impact on the success of the organisation. There are many examples of this in the car industry. Before its acquisition by Ford, Jaguar had a reputation for unreliability which severely impacted its image and sales prospects. Japanese cars, notably those produced by Toyota, have a reputation for product quality and this is an attractive element in their market offering. To quote one specific example, Mercedes designed a car, the Mercedes A Class for a more mass-market customer than its traditional offerings. However, it acquired a reputation in the late 1990s as being unstable which had a bad impact on the overall image of Mercedes. Product quality and perceived product quality is thus an important asset for any business.

Suppliers and associated business relationships

In recent years the relationships between firms in the supply chain have become increasingly complicated. In addition to the traditional relationships there has been the development of outsourcing and joint venturing on a scale without historic precedent. The totality of these relationships is a vital asset for a business. The development, for example, of just-in-time production has led to major improvements in terms of quality, flexibility and stock-holding levels for firms. These types of relationship may now be core to the competitive advantage of a wide range of business enterprises.

Customers

Another business trend in the past few years has been to pay greater attention to businesses' customers and to cater to them as individuals. Most organisations try to establish the profitability of each customer relationship and cater their policies around their perceptions of the customer value to an organisation. The 80–20 rule is often applied to customers in that 20 per cent of customers generate 80 per cent of profits. In my experience of banking, the 10–110 rule would be more appropriate – 10 per cent of customers generate 110 per cent of profits. Understanding customer values and basing policies on those values is an important element in sensible customer management. Businesses are vulnerable to key customer relationships. Robin Bellis-Jones, who has worked extensively in introducing activity-based costing systems to businesses, has suggested that many organisations' most important customers by value of transactions are likely to be unprofitable customers. The reason for this is that they demand a customised service and they will negotiate advantageous prices. Customers are a major source of risks for a business, but to understand the exact nature of the risks requires a high degree of sophistication in being able to measure the relationship.

Derek Wanless, the former chief executive of NatWest Bank, has argued that the competitive advantage that traditional banks have in comparison with new or potential industry entrants is in relation to the customer information that they have embedded in their systems because this will enable them to provide for customers in ways which are superior to those which can be achieved by any new entrant.

People

Sometimes people are considered as a key resource for organisations. Many see the chief executive or members of the board as irreplaceable and insure them for large amounts of money. Within organisations there is an increasing trend to undertake skills audits to ensure that the organisation has the requisite skills for its desired operations. Many businesses are complaining that they have too few people with project management skills. Succession planning and training to ensure that the business is not vulnerable to staff leaving or promoted within the organisation are vital to prevent shortages of key organisational skills.

Information systems

Information is a key resource for many businesses. The view from Derek Wanless cited above indicates how important information systems may prove to the running of businesses. The management, motivation and control systems of any organisation are vital to its success.

Processes and operational systems

A major revolution in business management has been the focus on processes and their improvement through more rational organisation and the exploitation of computer technology. These processes are seen as a vital element in the value chain for most businesses and it is important to look at them carefully to analyse what risks they might be subject to. The operational systems are the ways in which a businesses undertakes its activities and they are related to and overlap with the concept of processes.

Culture

A core resource of any organisation is its culture since it is a key determinant of how it actually operates. Let us take the example of Marks and Spencer, which was rated by John Kay in his *Foundations of Corporate Success* (1993, Oxford University Press) as the tenth most successful European company in the period 1981–90 in terms of adding value. It has a very strong internal culture and when we visited it as part of our MBA programme during this period myself and my colleagues were struck by the unique nature of the culture. There was a strong focus on all managerial staff having experience on the shop floor and having grown up in the Marks and Spencer way. The company was quite prepared to make its own decisions and to undertake business in ways different to all its competitors – for example, it did not at that time spend any money on TV advertising and sourced a high proportion of its clothing from the UK.

One factor which surprised me given my background in performance measurement was the simplicity with which the company approached these issues, although it did focus on what was selling in its individual outlets and departments. It was one of the last UK retailers to introduce computer point-of-sale technology and had difficulties in employing and assimilating IT staff since good IT staff did not have a career which included a spell on the shop floor in a retail environment. Our MBA group concluded that Marks and Spencer was an extremely effective organisation with a strong culture but saw it also as an authoritarian organisation with limited flexibility. We saw this as a vital culture for success in a stable environment but had doubts as to its ability to change were it to encounter a period of difficulty.

In the 1990s Marks and Spencers has seen a period of difficulty and has found it hard to adjust in relation to the competition. I saw this for myself when I went to a branch in an English provincial town at Christmas to buy some presents. I was there for 20 minutes and saw only one shopper under the age of 45. The company has had particular problems with its clothes retailing. Culture was a key element in its success and it has subsequently been an important hindrance in the company's ability to change.

This short case study illustrates the importance of culture and its benefits and defects. It is a key resource and thus needs to be considered explicitly. In the example of Bank One, an organisation which has developed through mergers and acquisitions, one sees a deliberate attempt to ensure that the culture is not diluted by this growth process.

Reputation

Reputation is a key resource of any business and one of the reasons why it can operate successfully. It is a resource that needs to be nurtured and can be harmed by a single event. Gerald Ratner's statement about the jewellery that his company sold (*see* p. 6) was sufficient to destroy his business and his career. It is said, for example, that Rothschild, the merchant bank, in evaluating any given business proposal asks how it might impact on its reputation for it sees reputation as a key asset. It is interesting to postulate whether Bill Gates' philanthropic activity goes some way to counterbalance the problems which his company Microsoft is encountering over the competition legalisation in the United States.

In trying to identify the risks to which an organisation or business is subject it is useful to consider what resources of the organisation are at risk. This can most easily be undertaken by looking at the strategic position of the organisation and how it hopes to be successful. The identification of the key resources is an important first step in risk identification.

HOW ARE THE RESOURCES OF THE BUSINESS AT RISK?

The identification of the resources of the business is easier to undertake than the task of identifying *how* the individual resources or categories of resource are at risk. Any attempted list must be regarded as tentative and is highly unlikely to be entirely comprehensive. A starting list of factors to consider in terms of the risks to a business's assets would be: organisation, people, inputs and outputs, processes and operational systems, external environment, gearing and financial markets. We will consider each of these categories individually.

Organisation

A business faces risks in terms of how adequately it is organised. The kind of factors which may lead to risks for an organisation relate to management, information, planning, and controls. The managerial structure can lead to confusion of responsibilities and risks to the businesses resources. It is important in setting up a sensible risk management system to ensure that there is clear responsibility for the management and identification of particular risks. That is why the Market Risk Amendment of the Basle-based International Bank of Settlements suggests that market risks should be isolated in a trading book which is separate from a bank's banking book to ensure market risks are clearly identified and responsibility for their management clearly allocated. The Market Risk Amendment also indicates that information systems should be set up to clearly identify market risk separately within a bank's information systems. There are many risks which will flow from poor information systems. One bank with which I worked had three measures of its deposits for a particular time period, all different, and this meant that in the resulting confusion it was difficult for the bank to have a sensible system for supporting its pricing decision. There has been a tendency for the proliferation of information systems within organisations, all measuring the same information from different perspectives for different organisational masters. These invariably lead to confusion and bad, risky management. The planning systems in terms of the budgetary and planning systems are vital tools for the co-ordination of activities within organisations. If these systems are poorly managed, it will expose the organisation to many important risks. Other types of risks can be the result of poor control systems – ensuring the quality through design and control of systems is a major element in avoiding the risks that result from poor quality.

People

People can be a major source of problems within an organisation. The story of Nick Leeson (*see* p. 57) is just a simple example of the possible risks that can be created by rogue staff who are not subject to adequate levels of control. It is often said that management would be easy if it was not for people. It is first of all important that individuals have the skills necessary for the jobs that they are expected to undertake – if they do not have the requisite skills and training, the organisation may be exposed to a great diversity of risks and problems.

A major possible source of accidents in organisations derives from the actions of individuals. There are a number of problems of this type discussed in *Accident and Design* (1996, UCL Press) edited by Christopher Hood and David K.C. Jones from which the following example is taken. The Chernobyl disaster in April 1986 was initiated in a test by the team in control of the reactor, who removed a number of layers of protection on a reactor which had serious design flaws. The way to avoid many accidents is to design systems which will be more independent of the errors of the individuals in charge of running them. Guarding against dishonesty is also vital for businesses – there are standard procedures to ensure that businesses are not defrauded. The attitudes and motivation of staff can have a major impact on the likelihood of problems since staff with poor morale are difficult to imbue with a consciousness of risk management. In the past few decades industrial disputes have become less prominent in relation to business risks but it is important that any business considers how it can manage the possibility of industrial disputes.

Inputs and outputs

A business may be highly dependent on the supply of certain inputs, so it is vital to have a sensible sourcing policy in terms of a number of suppliers and diversifying any risks in relation to supply. The quality of inputs and outputs can be another major risk issue for some businesses. If one considers high-quality restaurants, they have in general a problem in obtaining ingredients of a sufficiently high quality for their cooking.

The development of just-in-time production has been associated with improvements in the quality of inputs and the timing of deliveries. There have been many developments in relation to quality issues for business. We have insufficient space to focus on these issues within the confines of this book, but it is important to realise that quality control is a vital element in the whole risk management system for a business.

A major-output related risk with which I have been involved extensively in my professional life is in relation to new product launches. The overwhelming number of businesses have as part of their activity the launch of new products and these launches may involve very high degrees of risk. As part of the development project for any new product it is important to ensure risks are well analysed and that any possible system for reducing risk, provided it is worthwhile, is introduced.

Processes and operational systems

There are many problems that an organisation can face in the efficiency and continued operation of its systems. It is important to consider how an organisation might continue operation if there was a major disruption to its processes and operational systems. Contingency planning is a very important issue which has been highlighted in recent years with the development of IT. A good example is the Love Bug, a computer virus which was circulated around the globe in early May 2000 and which led to the shutdown of some vital internal computer systems in many large organisations.

External environment

In the long run many of the most important risks for a business emanate from its external environment, which is less easy to control and appears to change more rapidly that the internal environment.

The economy in which an organisation operates can have a major impact on its performance. The economy in this sense is that relevant to the operations of the business and may not just be that of an individual country. There are many risks from the economy that impact on market and credit risks, such as, for example, the level of interest rates. It is important not only to forecast but to evaluate risks which although they may not represent our best guess are still possible and are related to adverse outcomes.

The competitive environment has a major impact on a firm's operations. To use Porter's analytical categories it is necessary to consider the firms at the same position in the value chain, firms at other positions in the firm's current value chain, the producers of substitute products, and possible entrants and how they will be impacted by developments in technology. Many specific risks for businesses relate to the immediate competitive environment.

The regulatory environment is an important part of the environment in which any firm operates. There are many sectors, notably the financial sector and the utilities, where the operations of a business are subject to extensive controls from the state or appointed independent regulators. There is also the legal environment which is perpetually changing and will lead to a diversity of risks for businesses.

A significant example is the 1998 Human Rights Act which incorporated the European Convention of Human Rights into English law. Its introduction into English law in late 2000 will create many uncertainties over the legal obligations of firms until there is an established body of decided cases. It may entirely change the nature of UK law and certainly may create a diversity of risks for any business which operates in the UK.

Social changes can lead to changes in the patterns of demand for different products. Over the past few decades it has become progressively more socially unacceptable to wear fur garments. This has had a serious impact on the suppliers of this type of clothing. In addition, the ageing populations in most of the developed countries will have major impacts on how the national income is spent in the future.

Accidents and natural disasters can have a significant impact on the activities of an organisation. It is important, even if we are unable to isolate the nature of all these kinds of risk, that we have established contingency planning policies which allow the organisation to deal with any major problems from this source.

Gearing

The mechanism by which most businesses fail is that they run out of cash. The likelihood of this happening depends on the levels of cash commitments they have in any given time period. Gearing is a measure of the cash a business requires to continue its operations and therefore measures the risk of bankruptcy. The greater the likelihood of bankruptcy, the more difficult it is to operate a business. Suppliers and customers will change adversely their behaviour towards a business where there is a high expectancy of bankruptcy. The higher the level of gearing, the more expensive and difficult it will become to fund the business.

There are two types of gearing: operational and financial. They are measured in terms of Equation 8.1 and Equation 8.2. Financial gearing is the value of debt funding (Vd) for a business divided by the level of debt plus equity funding (Ve). It is the proportion of funding by debt. The debt needs to be serviced if the business is to continue. Eurotunnel, the company that manages the Channel Tunnel between the United Kingdom and France, and Eurodisney, the Paris-based theme park, would be examples of businesses which had problems in servicing their debt and were in reflection either poor business prospects or overgeared. Operational gearing is the ratio of fixed costs **FC** to variable costs **VC** plus fixed costs. The higher the level of operational gearing, the higher the level of revenue necessary to cover costs. Eurotunnel and Eurodisney would also be examples of businesses which were highly operationally geared.

Equation 8.1

$$\text{Financial gearing} = \frac{Vd}{Vd + Ve}$$

Equation 8.2

$$\text{Operational gearing} = \frac{FC}{FC + VC}$$

In one of the above sections we mentioned that new product launches were a source of risk for businesses. The higher the degree of operational risk in relation to a new product launch, the higher the risk of the new product launch.

Financial markets

The financial markets are the source of financial risks and in particular market risks. These risks need to be identified and dealt with. However, there are many other risks which emanate from the financial markets and they have to an extent been dealt with in terms of the economic environment. Exchange rates and interest rate risks may be integrally embedded in the operations of the organisation and they need to be identified and dealt with.

It is impossible to identify all the sources of risk but this set of categories can form the basis for a sensible risk identification procedure.

THE RISK MATRIX

In the previous two sections we have attempted to give a comprehensive view of what is at risk in an organisation and how it is at risk. The combination of these two sets of categories will form a matrix structure which can be used as a tool to identify risks. This structure is identified in Table 8.2. This can be seen as the basic tool for brainstorming in relation to the risks faced by the organisation. It can be used for brainstorming at the strategic level provided the process is accompanied by a strategic analysis of the organisation. It can also be used at the level of organisational units. The range of units for which it may be applied is outlined in Figure 8.1. There are choices as to what level of risk analysis to undertake and as to whether one wishes to extend it to all the possible risk units within an organisation. This will ultimately be a decision for top management in the light of their strategic evaluation of the risks which the organisation faces.

Table 8.2 The risk matrix

	What is at risk	Physical assets	Financial obligations	Performance	Inputs	Outputs	Suppliers	Business relationships	Customers	People	Information systems	Processes and operational systems	Culture	Reputation
How it is at risk														
Organisation														
Management														
Planning														
Information														
Controls														
People														
Skills														
Attitudes														
Dishonesty														
Control Systems														
Morale														
Industrial Relations														
Inputs and outputs														
Suppliers														
Quality														
Timeliness														
Reliability														
New Product Launches														
Processes and operational systems														
Breakdown														
Disruption														
Vulnerability														
External environment														
Economic														
Competitive														
Regulatory														
Legal														
Social														
Disasters														
Gearing														
Financial														
Operational														
Financial														
Asset prices														
Interest rates														
Exchange rates														
Commodity prices														
Credit risk issues														

Fig. 8.1 **Organisational units to which the risk identification process may be applied**

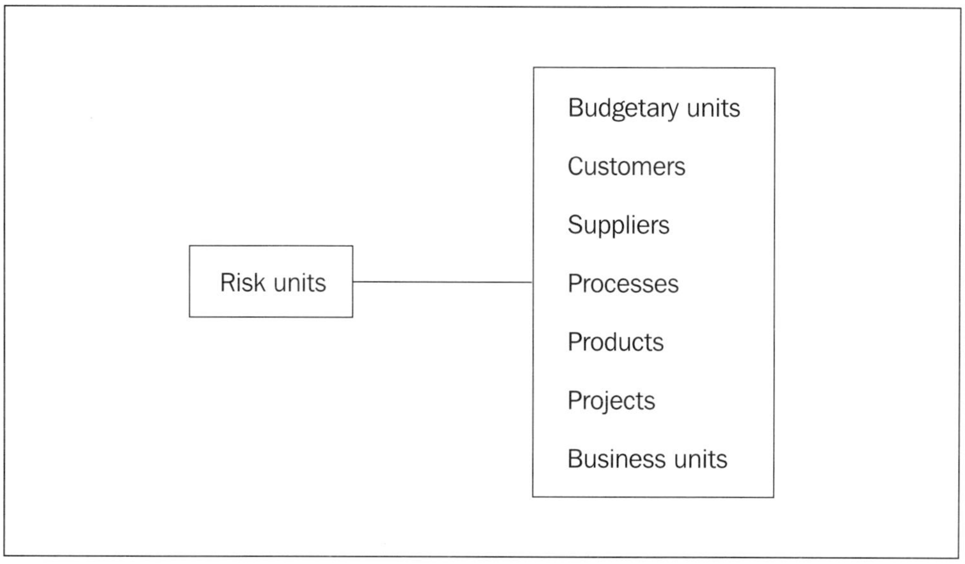

Although a risk evaluation gains value where it is applied comprehensively to an organisation, it can be applied independently to an individual risk unit. To take a simple example, if one is managing a project it would be good managerial practice to undertake a risk analysis of that project. This book also recommends that the establishment of an enterprise-wide risk management system is undertaken in stages, thus the process of risk identification should also take place in stages.

CONCLUSION

The identification of risk, particularly operational risk, is far from easy. There are many possible types and sources of risk. It is important to use the experience of other organisations and apply the expertise to be found in a diversity of risk-related disciplines. The overall identification of risk can benefit from the application of these essentially external perspectives. However, particularly for operational risk it is important for an organisation to try to brainstorm over its individual risks. This process needs to be accompanied by a strategic analysis which seeks to establish the key value-creating activities within the organisation. The 'what is at risk', 'how it is at risk' tool will aid in brainstorming. It will identify what is at risk even if it is not always the case that one can identify how it is at risk. It will also have to be put within a process which identifies risks in relation to a number of more specific risk-related disciplines.

9

Risk classification and management

INTRODUCTION

Having identified the risks it is important to try to organise what is a very diverse set of risks into some pattern which is amenable to management. This chapter tries to categorise the responses to the different types of risk and how they should be managed. The risks considered will be those established by the risk matrix system and any other process of risk identification.

RISK CLASSIFICATION

The use of the techniques outlined in the previous chapter will generate a wide diversity of results and separate identified risks. The process should be used to identify as many and as diverse a range of risks as possible. The identification of risks should be separated from the evaluation of the magnitude of the different risks. This is important since when brainstorming the different types of risks one wishes any sessions to be as free form as possible. Exploring magnitudes will tend to close down the discussion and it will be less fruitful than might otherwise be the case.

Having identified as many risks as possible they should be subjected to the technique for risk evaluation contained in Figure 9.1. This technique has been widely used by the US military in risk assessment and will decide which risks will need to be dealt with and which need not be dealt with. It is not entirely successful in identifying a set of risk priorities since there are also considerations of how easily or expensively the different types of risks can be managed. It is also necessary to consider whether there are certain risks which the organisation wishes to take as part of its activity, since one of the aspects of every business is that it is involved in risk taking.

Fig. 9.1 Categorising risks

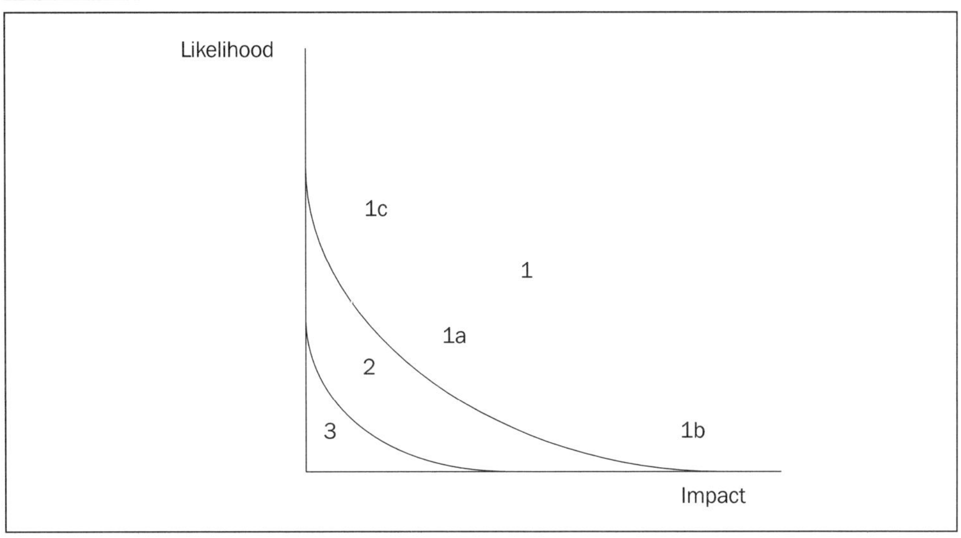

Risks can be classified in terms of their likelihood of occurrence and the level of their impacts. The latter may need to be analysed in terms of the more sophisticated management of risk discussed earlier. The risk categories give some indication of the urgency with which something should be done about the risks. Category 3 risks are of relatively small likelihood and impact, and many of these may safely be ignored since any policy must concentrate on those impacts which may be significant. Category 2 risks are of intermediate importance and should be considered only when policy has dealt with the most vital risks. The risks in category 1 are those which are very likely, those which are very significant, and some which are both likely and significant. The risks which are likely and significant should be the highest priority of risk; these are classified on the figure as 1a. Where they are likely but not significant, they need not be a key focus of policy; this is the case with risks in category 1c. Where risks are significant but not considered to be likely, they will probably be relegated to the second category of risks to be dealt with; these are labelled 1b. These risks are often the most difficult to deal with for policy purposes. If an organisation does not understand the nature of these risks, which may often be the case, they can be the risks which lead to most long-term difficulty. An example of these kinds of risks might be if a biologically engineered organism led to some devastating pollution problem.

It is likely that some of these risks will have to be regarded as so remote that an organisation will not focus on them in risk management policy. One must also add in conclusion that the classification of risks as 1b does not necessarily lead to a decision to eliminate those risks since they may be integral risks to the business undertaken by the organisation.

QUANTIFICATION OF RISKS

The quantification required for the analysis in the previous section does not need to be particularly elaborate and there is much debate as to the degree to which risks can be quantified. One should always try to give a numerical estimate of their importance at any given point in time, but there are certain risks for which this should never be taken too seriously since we do not always have a good knowledge of the quantitative aspects of risks even when we can make some estimate of their magnitude.

RESPONSES TO RISK

Responses to risk management can be divided into the following categories: accept the risk; insure against the outcomes; reduce the likelihood by, in the main, quality and process control; reduce the impacts in terms of contingency planning; and hedge the worst outcomes.

Accept the Risk

There are certain business-related risks which no enterprise will seek to eliminate. They will certainly wish to manage the organisation as well as possible in the face of those business uncertainties, but they will always wish to be subject to some risk since that is the way in which the business or organisation fulfils its objectives or adds value. These are the risks which the equity holder takes. It may be sensible to adjust the funding of the business to cover what are seen to be the levels of risk. Microsoft has no outstanding debt and $18 billion in cash. This can be seen as an important buffer against risk.

Insurance

Practically all organisations hold insurance in relation to some risks. They many insure their property or against certain contingencies. In recent years the development of credit derivatives has formed a type of insurance against credit risks. It is rarely the case that large organisations will insure against all insurable risks since they may be able, if they are sufficiently large, to spread their risks and save any margin the insurance industry makes on premia. Many companies insure against major loss events and take the risks if they can benefit internally through diversification.

BP, the oil group, is an interesting case. In the 1980s it paid $115 million in premia per annum and received $25 million per annum in claims. In reviewing its position it thought that insurance providers could price and compete well where the risks were standard but they did not necessarily assess risk or price effectively for risks which were large and non-standard. BP decided to take any risks which were larger than $10 million. It thought that these big losses were such that they could be adequately absorbed by shareholders. Thus it decided to let its shareholders take on the risks which were in essence specific to the business and could be hedged out by shareholders' portfolios. On average it thought the shareholders would gain from the lower premia. It was, in fact, seeking to benefit from what it thought was mispricing by the insurance industry.

An interesting example in relation to insurance is that of Honeywell, the US diversified manufacturer, which in 1997 replaced its separate insurance contracts for a number of separate categories of risk with a single contract of cover for aggregate losses over these categories.

Reduce the likelihood of bad outcomes

Many of the risks that organisations face come from the integrity of processes or controls. If one considers the diversity of categories of risk it is possible to design a process which will lower the risk of failure and in many cases eliminate certain types of risk. The failure to separate Nick Leeson's trading from the recording of those trades was a vital process flaw within Barings' control systems. The diversity of this point can be indicated by taking the example of Gerald Ratner, where if his speeches and public utterances had been subject to scrutiny by a PR function, be it internal or external, he would have been far less likely to describe his firm's products as 'crap'. Therefore the main type of policy to reduce the likelihood of many risks turning bad is to institute sensible risk-based processes. The focus of the Turnbull Report is to manage risk by an embedded control system.

Contingency planning

There is not adequate space in this book to cover in detail many perspectives of contingency planning. A good practical guide to the topic is Kenneth Myers' *Managers' Guide to Contingency Planning for Disasters* (1999, John Wiley). In this book he divides the different perspectives for contingency planning into four phases. Firstly, prevention, and preparedness training. Preparedness training includes planning and some exercises related to possible disasters. The nature of disaster may be difficult to forecast but the impacts one is trying to deal with should be identifiable. The initial response to a disaster in the first 24–48 hours should be based on an emergency-response document. It should identify issues such as employee and customer communication, damage assessment, establishing communications and IT, physical security, and any required reallocations. The next phase involves the focus on the protecting of cashflows since the major problem for the business is if it were to run out of cash. The final phase relates to restoring facilities and returning to normal operations. The key is to ensure that the business survives the catastrophe and this is related to ensuring in the crisis that as far as possible the immediate and long-term future of the business is secured.

Hedging

There are a number of ways in which an organisation's risks can be hedged. It is possible to hedge some lines of business by putting other business lines with them in a single organisation. In general, unless there are other gains or synergies, as for example in terms of tax benefits or general synergies, the shareholder can in many cases replicate these types of hedges and there is no particular reason why the business should undertake them. There are many hedges which can be applied, especially to market risks, and these may have benefits for the business, for example, in terms of hedging interest rate or exchange rate risks. If there is an extensive analytical requirement to understand the nature of the risks faced by an organisation, it is likely to create hedges for risk which are unlikely to be replicated by shareholders.

It is important that having identified the major risks faced by an organisation and categorised these in terms of where the priorities for risk management should be put, each type of risk is considered by those most professional in its management and a decision is made to accept or manage the risks.

CONCLUSION

It is important to establish the risk management system of a business in a coherent framework. Coherence will ensure that as few potential problems as possible are ignored within the risk management framework. The identification and the consideration of how risks will be managed is an essential element in establishing this enterprise-wide risk management system.

10

The organisational perspective of risk management

INTRODUCTION

This chapter deals with the organisational perspective of risk management. It considers the establishing of an enterprise-wide risk management system. There are, of course, many different types of organisations to which a risk management system can be addressed and this section will not be appropriate for every type of organisation. Some will be more heavily dependent on established types of risk management systems, for example in relation to financial risks or insurance risks. Others will be subject to key health and safety management-based systems. Thus any of the points made in this chapter may need to be adapted to a particular organisation. It is not a blueprint, it is a set of considerations to condition policy.

ESTABLISHING AN ENTERPRISE-WIDE RISK MANAGEMENT SYSTEM

As with any major managerial initiative it is necessary that a risk management system, if it is to be taken seriously by the organisation, must be seen to have the approval of top management. The importance of these systems in the current climate means that they should be seen to be initiated with the wholesale support of the chief executive. An excellent start to this process is to make a board member responsible for risk management and if it is seen to be their key responsibility, risk management will be regarded as having vital importance within the organisation. It is certainly the mantra of all project management that if the project is expected to have a major influence, appropriate sponsorship and ongoing interest must be forthcoming. It is also important to say that many projects have formal approval and interest, but for this project to work it is imperative that the interest is not just token – an ongoing, active interest which convinces the organisation that this is important and not 'just something to be seen to be doing'.

To set up an enterprise-wide risk management system is a major project for any organisation and it should be managed in the way that any major project is managed. A multidisciplinary team should be established, drawn from within the organisation – the virtue of this is that a range of skills can be used for the project and the team can exploit their contacts within the organisation. If organisations do not have extensive knowledge of risk management it is important to ensure that the correct skills are deployed. This may involve outside recruitment or external consultancy. However, it is important to manage this process so that the business is not the subject of the application of a standard consultancy methodology. Each organisation is different and consultancy methodologies are not necessarily correct, even where they have been successfully applied in other organisations.

There is extensive evidence that the applying of a risk management methodology to an organisation will benefit from a pilot project whose methodology can subsequently be applied to the whole organisation. This will enable a project team to be assembled and bedded down and the methodology employed to be tested and honed within a particular organisational environment. It is important to see any pilot project in terms of a building block for the future, so decisions made and validated at that stage will have a major impact on the way the project is 'rolled out' within the organisation generally.

Let us look at an example of the methodology employed by Amelia Financial Systems for the development of enterprise-wide operational risk systems. The company sees the process for developing an operational risk system in the terms illustrated in Table 10.1. Although this structure was designed to provide a systematic overview of a process for establishing a system for operational risk, it forms a useful framework for discussion of establishing a more general system for risk management. Each of the stages can be considered and modified to establish the more general framework. This set of categories should not be seen as stages for a project to follow in chronological order but rather as a categorisation of the major considerations which need to be addressed by the project. To take an example, communication will be vital to the success of ensuring that all staff understand their role in risk management and thus will need to be a major ongoing consideration.

Table 10.1 Amelia Financial Systems' operational risk programme

A staged approach to establishing risk management systems
Planning and communication
Risk framework
Risk identification and assessment
Core reporting
Policy formulation and insurance review
Advanced systems integration
Complex risk quantification and capital application

Planning and communication

Initial research for the project should focus on what is the best practice generally and which issues are relevant to the particular sector or industry of the organisation. This should form the conditioning knowledge on which the project should be planned and organised.

The first stage of the process is the initial planning, which will define the nature of the project. It is in essence the preparing of a business plan for the project which will provide the basis for evaluation as to whether the project is worthwhile for the organisation. It will be a strategic and financial plan of the impact of the project within the business. The process of validation of the plan will entail convincing the key executive personnel as to the necessity of the system for the business and motivating them to give sufficient backing to ensure the project is successful.

The establishment of an enterprise-wide risk management system is only the most concrete and visible embodiment of what should be a major cultural initiative within the business. It is an overarching perspective which spans the operations and quality management within the whole organisation. It is thus vital to see communication as a key element in the project's success.

Risk framework

There will, in any large organisation, be certain organisational units which deal with risk and risk-related issues. These may be related to internal audit, account management, or treasury management, to name but a few examples. Each of these organisational units will have its own framework, body of knowledge, systems, procedures and culture. They will need to be related to the project since the risks which they consider are a vital element in the totality of organisational risks. There are many organisations which, for example, have based their operational risk management within the internal auditing function, and the salaries of auditors have increased in recent years, reflecting the increasing importance of risk management. The organisation must deal with any political issues surrounding these groups since they have important vested interests which will be affected by the establishment of an enterprise-wide risk management system. As with any project, care should be taken to ensure that the politics are well managed and this will be an area of potential political conflict.

As part of implementing the enterprise-wide risk management system there will be a need to establish a system of risk management and control. This is so important that it will be the subject of a major section on what is a sensible framework for organisational risk management. We thus do not consider the general issues in relation to the ongoing structure of risk management within this section.

In order to establish a sensible enterprise-wide risk management system it is important to review how risk is currently dealt with within the organisation and to undertake an audit as to the degree to which it may be improved and integrated with any new systems. This type of audit should form one of the exercises as a prelude to the drawing up of an initial business plan for validation of the proposal. The plan should deal with the integration and upgrading of any existing systems and procedures.

Providing a framework should ensure that a comprehensive view is taken of risk management. In many banking organisations, risks are managed within a framework where separate management is established for market, credit and operational risks, and these management positions will report to a head of risk who will in some instances be a member of the board. In terms of systems development the separation of credit and market risks from operational risk systems would normally be the case.

Risk identification and assessment

Market and credit risk assessment will in general be the province of risk experts in these two fields. If one considers operational risk, there is no one given body of expertise and knowledge which can be applied to risk identification and assessment. There is, however, a diversity of areas of knowledge that need to be applied, for example in terms of engineering risk, hazard identification and insurance. Thus to deal with operational risk is more difficult and complicated.

We have already discussed the operational risk systems at Bankers Trust and how risks were identified on the basis of a centralised analysis benefiting from both internal and external information. Whatever risk identification process is chosen there will probably be an element which incorporates risk identification workshops. Certainly there will be workshops on strategic risk identification for executive management. There is also an increasing desire within the banking industry to establish databases similar to those in the airline industry which focus on crashes and near misses. The trend in many institutions is to identify risks partly centrally and partly through a process of workshops with line operational management. If, for example, one is identifying operational risk, the use of the risk matrix outlined in Table 8.2 is a vital tool for this type of workshop. The choice of risk identification process may be for individual businesses but it is increasingly being moved from a centralised to a line-based process.

The risk assessment should be separated from the assessment. If one is collecting part of this information by line workshops, the two exercises should be formally separated, even if carried out in the same session. The assessment can be undertaken in terms of the 1a, 1b, 1c, 2, 3 processes outlined in the last chapter. In fact, this process can be aggregated over the hierarchical structure of the enterprise. It can be augmented by estimates of the quantitative financial impact and likely probability associated with particular risks. These quasi-subjective estimates may prove useful guidance in risk evaluation. Having evaluated the risks it is then useful to ask workshop members to outline how these most important risks are currently managed, how they could be better managed, and where one may derive extra information on the management of these risks.

It should always be borne in mind that the workshop process will have its flaws. Line management is often too close to problems to have an entirely objective vision of their nature. Organisational structure creates problems as well as solving them. The benefits of a process perspective have always been related to the problems which organisational structure may create. It is thus important to try to provide a process, product and business unit perspective to any risk analysis.

In conclusion, risk identification and assessment may be based on the information that resides within an organisation, but one must always approach this information from a critical perspective and realise that there is important knowledge and practice external to the organisation which should be included in any excellent enterprise-wide risk management system.

Core reporting

Establishing and running a risk management system is a process of continual learning. The risks are diverse, sometimes changing, and in many cases very complicated to understand. The measurement of risk exposure or performance at a particular point in time may be inexact, yet in some instances very precise. Thus there are problems over what one should report about the nature of risks in a particular situation. The lack of an academically satisfactory definition of risk for use in risk management led to the development of the concept of value at risk. Whatever may be the ideal index of measurement and reporting in relation to risk, one is sure that the risk identification process will indicate that the information is either not collected or not easily available within an organisations systems. One should as a general principle measure what is available and use surrogates, some of which will not be entirely satisfactory. The establishment of a core reporting system with interfaces with other risk management systems is vital.

Any core risk management system should be seen as work in progress and thus should be subject to continual review. These developments take time; they need to respond to internal organisational changes and the improvement in our understanding of the different risk based processes.

Policy formulation and insurance review

The risk identification and assessment process will be a prelude for an evaluation of how the risks should be dealt with. This can take a number of forms. Initially it entails deciding in what ways the various risks will be taken on and managed. As part of this process there will be an evaluation of whether various insurable risks need to be insured against. There are many risks, most notably financial ones, that need to be considered in terms of not only how they should be managed but also the process by which it is decided to take a risk and the structure of limits which should be applied to those risks.

Advanced systems integration

The linking of risk-related systems is important in the development of a sophisticated risk management system for an enterprise. To give an example, if one considers a banking organisation initiating a loan for a customer, this will have an impact on a number and range of risk-based systems. The likely impacts are outlined in Figure 10.1, which indicates only the impacts on risk-based systems. The decision of whether to extend a loan to a customer is likely to be based on the credit evaluation process, which will involve an evaluation of the customer and loan application and a review of the customer's behaviour in relation to other products. Thus the loan evaluation decision will require the use of a primary risk management system within the organisation. The more sophisticated banking institutions have customer value or profitability systems.

Fig. 10.1 Impacts on risk systems from a customer loan

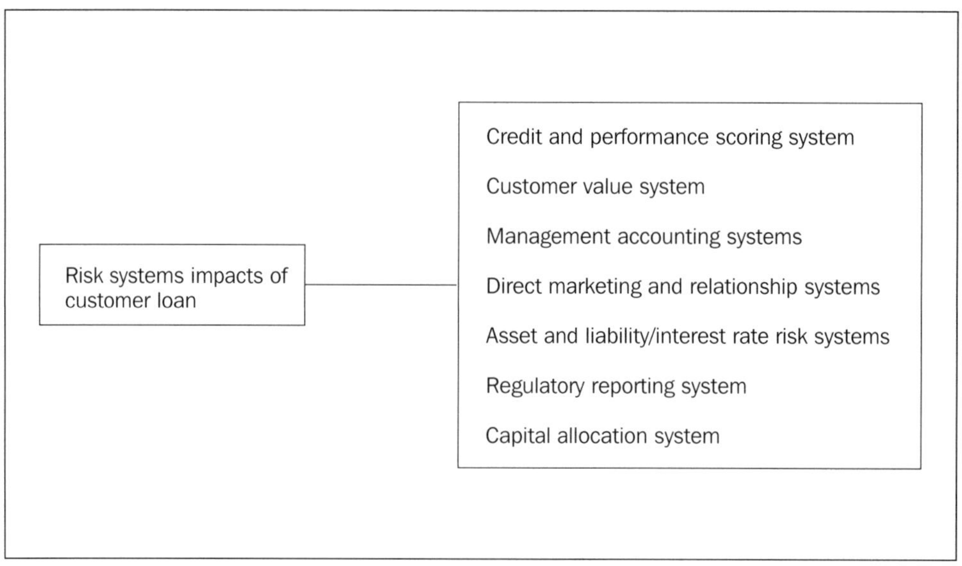

American Express, for example, can evaluate the customer in terms of the financial returns they are expected to generate for the organisation within the next five years. The evaluation of how the loan is likely to impact on the organisation will form part of the decision whether to extend credit or not. The management accounting system will incorporate the loan within the structure of accounts and reporting of the bank. The credit limits will be updated. There will be allocations to products, underwriters, organisational units and so on. It will be part of the risk analysis and monitoring of each of those units to which it applies. The impacts in terms of customer values and scoring systems will form a basis for the direct marketing systems and those systems that may govern customer relations. The loan will have an impact on the nature of assets and liabilities held by the bank and will thus have to become an input to the asset and liability management systems, especially with a focus on the understanding, management and reporting of interest rate risks. The numbers to be reported to the key financial regulators will also have to be updated. Most major banking organisations have a system of capital allocation in order to ensure that the risks which they undertake provide sufficient return and these systems will be impacted by the loan and its behaviour.

The sale of a single loan is therefore an important example of the way in which complicated reporting and analytical risk-based systems are related. The objective to which a system of enterprise-wide risk management should be dedicated is to provide a situation by which these different risk-based systems can be integrated into a comprehensive risk management system.

Complex risk quantification and capital allocation

If one considers all the disciplines, both scientific and financial, for understanding the nature of risk, in most cases they will provide a quantitative analysis of the risks of a certain type that an organisation faces. They may be aggregated to provide numbers such as value at risk, which may prove valuable to management, but whether aggregated or not it is important to provide the analytical framework within which risks can be reported and managed.

Capital allocation is a technique used in the financial industry to decide if there is an appropriate return for undertaking a risky activity. It sees the basic function of capital as providing a buffer against which extraordinary losses are registered. The capital is usually allocated on the basis of a value at risk measurement of losses. The return is divided by the capital at risk in an activity. In general, the approach of regulators is to believe that these systems in relation to market risk are satisfactory, but they do not seem prepared as yet to accept them for credit or operational risks. While in general I approve the vision that the taking of risks by a business should be compensated by an adequate return, I am not convinced about the validity of these types of system. The discussion of the issues can be found in my next book, *Transfer Pricing for Financial Institutions*, to be published by Gresham Publications in conjunction with the Chartered Institute of Bankers. These types of system are difficult to design and need to be the subject of expert advice and consideration. In the sections above I have indicated some support for CAPM-based systems.

While the above indicates the process for the setting up of an enterprise-wide risk management system it is far from a detailed outline of the process. If one were to give some advice in the setting up of these projects it would be that the more care that is taken at the front end, the more satisfactory will be the results. It is easier to define the parameters of the system at the beginning rather than changing the process half-way through. It is vital also to make use of best practice wherever it may be found, especially that relating to a particular industry.

THE ORGANISATIONAL STRUCTURE OF RISK MANAGEMENT

Having established a system of risk management it is vital to give it a managerial perspective. The important principle is to make the responsibilities of individuals and groups clear in terms of their role in risk management. There needs to be articulation of responsibilities in relation to specific risks – the process by which an organisation initiates risk, the ways in which it can be managed, and the nature of the reporting. The key elements in the process can be seen in Table 10.2, which will form the basis for considering the operational structure of a business from a risk management perspective. The first column looks at the risk responsibilities in relation to the standard management structure of the organisation. The key figures have other major roles but must be aware of what their risk-related responsibilities should be. The second column looks specifically at the risk-related structure in the organisation. The final column looks at some risk-related structures which will not be required by most enterprises but may form a vital role in some specific types of business enterprises.

Fig. 10.2 The key roles in the risk management process

Standard operational structure	*Risk structure*	*Ad hoc*
Board of directors	Risk management	Alco
Audit committee	Risk-based committee structure	Credit committee
Chief executive		
Senior executive management		
Line managers		

Board of directors

The boards of directors of public companies are being seen progressively as having a key risk management responsibility. There is an increasing focus worldwide to provide risk standards for all large businesses – to name but a few, 'Guidance on Assessing Control', CAN/CSA-Q850-97 by the Canadian Institute of Chartered Accountants; AS/NZS 4360:1999 applied to Australia and New Zealand; the Turnbull Report on internal control prepared by a working party of the Institute of Chartered Accountants in England and Wales and endorsed by the London Stock Exchange.

Responsibility for risk management is becoming a key role for boards of directors. The London Stock Exchange's Combined Code on Corporate

Governance, principle D.2, states that: 'The board should maintain a sound system of internal control to safeguard shareholders' investment and the company's assets.' Provision D.2.1 states that: 'The directors should, at least annually, conduct a review of the effectiveness of the group's system of internal control and should report to shareholders that they have done so. The review should cover all controls, including financial, operational and compliance controls and risk management.'

As a general principle the board should review these issues whether it is in a jurisdiction where it is forced to do so or not, since it is now an element in good management practice. Their roles are quite formal and it is important that the board be seen as having a key part in establishing and maintaining a system and culture which deals with the risks an organisation faces. These formal roles relate to an auditing type of function, but risk management should be more than that and it should ensure that there are sufficient returns for the risks which the organisation is prepared to take.

Audit committee

The audit committee plays a key role in considering whether the risk identification and management processes within the organisation are adequate. In essence, many major risk-related issues will be dealt with by the operations of this committee. It is essential that many operational risk problems will form a basis for the committee's deliberations.

Chief executive

The role of the chief executive officer (CEO) is central to the establishing and maintaining of an enterprise-wide risk management system. The chief executive gives the organisational focus on what is crucial to the operations of the business. In particular two facets tend to be central to the CEO role – ensuring that the organisation is risk vigilant, and ensuring that the organisation receives an adequate return for the risks it undertakes. There must be a focus on ensuring that risks are professionally identified and managed, and that there are clear managerial responsibilities to ensure that all aspects of risk management are adequately dealt with.

Senior executive management

In general, senior executive management perform within their individual roles one which is similar to that of the chief executive. It is important that they recognise their responsibilities and ensure that risk management within their sphere of operations is dealt with professionally.

Line managers

Many key risk responsibilities will devolve to line management. The operations of the business and operational risk management will often be linked to specific line managers. It is important for line managers to realise that their risk responsibilities should extend to the interfaces between their responsibilities and those of other line managers. There will be risks which are less easy to manage within any organisational structure since they fall between responsibilities. It is essential that the culture and accountabilities try as extensively as possible to deal with this type of problem.

Risk management

Increasingly there is a debate as to whether most businesses should have a risk director. It is a post which will give the appropriate impetus and prestige to risk management if one wishes to embed a risk culture within an organisation. The decision as to whether one should appoint such a manager depends on the type of business and the role of risk management in that business. It also depends on the other perspectives and requirements for the organisation. However, it is important to have a responsible manager for risk management supported by an adequate staff to undertake the requisite tasks.

The key to the risk management function is that it should be independent of the business units so that it can provide a view on risk issues which is not influenced by the requirements of business unit management. Establishing it in a separate hierarchy reporting to a risk director is a good mechanism for guaranteeing this level of independence. There may, however, be some risk-related staff in the operational units, for example, treasury risk management will tend to be within the treasury operation but independent from the front office and it is usually seen as a back-office function.

Another issue in establishing a risk management function is whether it should be independent from the auditing function. In general, the arguments for independence are more convincing. Auditing has a tradition which makes it focus on inspections and reports, which give a snapshot of issues. It is based on accounting skills which give auditing a certain culture and perspective. The broader range of analytical skills required for understanding the diversity of risk will not necessarily be possessed by auditing staff. In general, auditors provide an important risk management function but one is uneasy with them fulfilling all of the risk management functions.

It is important that coherence be given to risk management and having a risk management staff can provide that coherent overview, but risk management cannot always be undertaken by the risk management staff on their own. If one wishes to have a certain risk profile in relation to treasury management, for example, it is necessary for risk management to work in the development of trading strategies and limits but it is the treasury function which implements these policies. With many operational risks the line management of process will be vital to risk management; this again will not be undertaken by the risk managers.

Risk-based committee structure

Increasingly, businesses see a key role in risk management as that which can be performed by the risk management committee. This committee reports to the board of directors and is responsible for the overall management of risk within the business. The central responsibilities of the committee can be seen in terms of the suggestion by Robin Kendall, to develop, review, approve and monitor the strategies and exposure of the business to risks in conjunction with the company's board of directors. The membership of the committee can vary, but one should consider the following suggestions. The chairman should be an important member of the board and in particular a non-executive director. The committee should also contain the chief finance officer. The other members of the committee should depend on the organisation in question, but the chief legal officer, compliance officer and head of audit, as well as the senior risk manager, may be vital. It is also important that some members of the group have sufficient knowledge to understand the technical issues in relation to risk. Many of the problems concerning risk management were, in part, the result of organisational top management not being aware of the nature of the risks which the business was taking. Thus in deciding on the membership it is important to consider not just the organisational interests that should be represented but also the technical skills which will be useful to the committee.

In a large business which may be established as a set of companies a single risk management committee will not be entirely adequate to cover all the general risk issues and it may therefore be necessary to have a hierarchy of committees. These committees should be, to a degree, independent of the operational entities in which they are located and it may be useful if their reporting structure is through the main group risk management committee to the board. This will build on the issue that the risk management committees need to have influence and independence in relation to the operational units.

It is becoming a central prerequisite of risk management to have a policies and procedures manual, which is an outline of the main policies on the risk management of the business. They should be up to date and reviewed regularly. It will initially provide some degree of institutional audit on policies but will be the repository of an overview of what is required in policy terms within the organisation. The risk management function and the risk management committee will be the key players in the development of the manual.

Alco

In a study for the Bank Administration Institute, Barrett F. Binder and Thomas Lindquist (1982, *Asset-Liability Handbook*, Rolling Meadows, IL), found a high level of agreement among bankers that the Asset and Liability Committee, or Alco, was 'the single most important management group and function in the bank'. It is a central risk management committee and function within the banking industry. Its role is the co-ordinated management of the bank's balance sheet to allow the management of interest rate, liquidity and prepayment risk. This would be undertaken by matching the balance sheet repricing characteristics of assets and liabilities, off and on-balance sheet hedging with derivatives, and securitisation which will remove risks from the balance sheet. The Alco is thus a vital risk management function and committee within banking institutions.

Credit committee

The credit committee is often found in banking institutions and is focused on the management of credit risk within the bank's activities. It will review the whole range of credit risk in relation to lending, derivatives obligations, payments and transactions generally. The area of policy management in relation to credit risk from lending procedures, to the management of bad debt will be the ambit of this type of committee.

A RISK CULTURE

One of the most pervasive generalisations about groups is that they may be less risk averse than individuals. There is evidence that individuals also may suppress sensible evaluations of risk when it is in their own self-interest. Among smokers, for instance, there has never been a conviction that the link between smoking and illness was one for which there was a high degree of evidential support. Peter Swartz, an expert in scenario planning, cites IBM and Sears Roebuck's investment in Prodigy, the US banking investment in South America in the 1980s, and the fall of Long Term Capital Management in 1998, despite the presence of Nobel laureates as examples of smart people and companies making poor decisions since they did not challenge the strategic assumptions which they were making. They badly misjudged the risks of their situation.

There is important and conclusive evidence that individuals and groups will not adequately consider risks unless their activities are embedded in a culture which realises that bad outcomes do happen and it is being unprofessional not to adequately attempt to identify and deal appropriately with these risks. It is thus important that although an organisation or part of an organisation may have a view on the risks they face, their attitudes are continually challenged in an open environment which allows individuals to raise issues.

One example of the risk culture is in how open an organisation is or the degree of blame which is attached to failure. The airline industry is the archetype of these sorts of issues. In order to learn about the nature of risks there is a culture of reporting any near misses. If this culture is to work, those involved in near misses should not be penalised. An open risk-reporting culture is one in which blame does not result from openness. Another perspective to this issue is that a sensible risk management system will allocate responsibility for risk management to those who in principle can control the risks. Accountability is associated with incentives and penalties. The decision as to which of these paradigms is appropriate for risk management within a particular unit needs to be taken in terms of an understanding of the nature of risks and motivation in the unit. There is no uniform answer to the question. If there are important generalities, they would relate to how important it is to learn about risks, whether the reporting of near misses is a valuable element in this process, what motivates individuals and whether their actions will be altered if they are held responsible for errors in risk management.

An organisation which manages risks well needs to see risk as a key element in its activities. It needs to relate risks to the jobs of individuals. Those individuals need to see their roles within a risk perspective. They need to understand the risks they face and ensure that they are adequately managed. They should also be aware that changing activities and circumstances require vigilance in the identification and management of risk. Risk management is ultimately an individual responsibility.

CONCLUSION

This chapter has dealt with a number of practical risk issues. In essence, each organisation needs to consider risk from its individual perspective and although there may be guidelines to the particular line of business, all organisations face a different uncertain future with a different strategy and set of policies. However, it is vital to put in place an adequate identification, management and monitoring strategy for risk which impinges on the job of each individual in the organisation.

Section 4

Conclusions

11

Conclusions

Although there are standard definitions and categorisations of risk, the risks of a business are diverse, unique and always changing. The responsibility of executive managers is to ensure that risk management is professionally undertaken, and this will both raise returns and lower the volatility of the business.

Sensible risk management will enhance the value of the business. It is important to see risk management in terms of applying a number of specialist skills to appropriate risks and to also have a general risk management system which will cater for all the organisational risks for which there are not general specialist skills.

Co-ordination of risk identification, measurement and management will always prove difficult, and the allocation of managerial responsibilities should be clear and comprehensive. Establishing an enterprise-wide risk management system is now seen as an essential attribute of the good management of any large enterprise.

The main argument for establishing a risk management system is that it will enhance an organisation's value.